ENTREPRENEURIAL
LEADERSHIP

ENTREPRENEURIAL LEADERSHIP

The Art of Launching New Ventures,
Inspiring Others, and Running Stuff

JOEL PETERSON

HarperCollins
Leadership

AN IMPRINT OF HARPERCOLLINS

Published by HarperCollins Leadership, an imprint of HarperCollins Focus LLC.

Any internet addresses, phone numbers, or company or product information printed in this book are offered as a resource and are not intended in any way to be or to imply an endorsement by HarperCollins Leadership, nor does HarperCollins Leadership vouch for the existence, content, or services of these sites, phone numbers, companies, or products beyond the life of this book.

ISBN 978-1-4002-1677-2 (Ebook)

ISBN 978-1-4002-1675-8 (HC)

Library of Congress Cataloging-in-Publication Data

Names: Peterson, Joel, 1947- author.

Title: Entrepreneurial leadership : the art of launching new ventures, inspiring others, and running stuff / Joel Peterson.

Description: Nashville: HarperCollins Leadership, 2020.

Summary: "Make a lasting impact by launching new initiatives, inspiring others, and championing innovative approaches with this from-the-trenches guide by trusted executive mentor, entrepreneur, and leadership expert Joel Peterson"-- Provided by publisher.

Identifiers: LCCN 2019040207 (print) | LCCN 2019040208 (ebook) | ISBN 9781400216758 (hardcover) | ISBN 9781400216772 (ebook).

Subjects: LCSH: Entrepreneurship. | Leadership.

Classification: LCC HB615 .P39468 2020 (print) | LCC HB615 (ebook) | DDC

658.4/092--dc23

LC record available at https://lccn.loc.gov/2019040207

LC ebook record available at https://lccn.loc.gov/2019040208

Printed in the United States of America

20 21 22 23 LSC 10 9 8 7 6 5 4 3 2 1

To My Students

CONTENTS

FOREWORD

I first met Joel Peterson in 2010. I'd recently ended my military service, and I had been asked to consider joining the board of JetBlue, where Joel is the chairman. Before the board extended an official invitation, I was asked to meet individually with a few directors, so we could assess whether I'd be the right fit.

Upon sitting down with Joel, I was first struck by how humble and empathetic he was. In a one-on-one meeting, you get the sense he's thinking deeply about what he can do to help the person sitting across from him feel most comfortable and let his or her best qualities shine through. This may sound like a simple thing, but when you experience it in person, it's quite remarkable.

From the moment I attended my first board meeting, Joel embraced and mentored me. He recognized that despite my military leadership experience, I had a lot to learn about how corporations work. What's most striking about Joel in this setting is how quietly (but effectively) he guides a group of high-powered, sometimes voluble directors. He doesn't want or need anyone to recognize that he's in charge. He knows where he wants to go, but rarely does anyone recognize his hand on the tiller. The verb I often use to describe Joel is that he "shapes" things. When Joel is leading people, the group feels a unique sense of pride and accomplishment, because Joel deflects all credit away from himself and toward them. Joel epitomizes the selfless, self-effacing, servant leader—an operating style from which many of us can learn.

In *Entrepreneurial Leadership*, Joel lays out his vision for why the world needs more of these selfless, other-directed types. These are people who demonstrate the ability to do four things: build trust, set a mission, secure a team, and deliver results. Many people can do one or two of these things; remarkably few can do all of them. In this book, Joel offers practical guidance to help people on their journey to becoming an entrepreneurial leader.

This message resonates with me. During my years in the US Army, sometimes people asked me to comment on the general quality of our military commanders. Here's how I'd break it down: A very small percentage were incompetent, and how they managed to stay in their jobs was always a bit of a mystery. The overwhelming majority were extremely capable. If given the right rules and procedures, some supervision, and a good team, they could move an organization forward. (I call these leaders "mechanics"; in Joel's parlance, they are "presiders.") But only a very small percentage could really change an organization, particularly in an atmosphere with as much bureaucracy as exists in the armed forces. These few are the entrepreneurial leaders Joel is describing.

As a West Point graduate, I have a deep admiration for the military's ability to build leaders—especially the kind that excel at inspiring, engaging, and energizing subordinates. But I sometimes worry that the rules, formality, and bureaucracy of military life and training serve to file away whatever natural entrepreneurial edge our young officers may have. This is unfortunate, and it's partly why change in the military happens so slowly. Like most organizations, the US military would be better off if it had more entrepreneurial leaders.

Joel epitomizes these qualities to such an extent that I've sometimes made a statement my military friends think is hyperbole—but one I stand by. Here's the proposition: Ordinarily, officers spend at least twenty years being trained and reviewed for sequential promotions before attaining the rank of general, because the complexity of the job is thought to require a lifetime of on-the-job training. (This is why the army, unlike a corporation, doesn't use search firms or make external, mid-career hires.) But if Joel were somehow magically turned into a general and asked to lead infantry soldiers tomorrow, despite having no military experience, I'm certain he'd excel at the task. (Yes, we'd have to teach him how to salute, how to understand the army's arcane acronyms, and some basics of military strategy and tactics, but that wouldn't take long.) Joel would succeed because he knows how to problem solve, how to execute, how to motivate, how to coach, how to connect with people of any rank—and how to change organizations. Most importantly, soldiers would love being led by someone like Joel, just as I've loved being led and mentored by him during my postmilitary excursion into the business world.

In short, Joel Peterson excels at entrepreneurial leadership—and this book can teach you to excel at it too.

—General Stanley A. McChrystal,
US Army, Retired
Alexandria, Virginia

INTRODUCTION

A NIGHT ALONE
ON THE MOUNTAIN

*Not till we are lost, in other words, not till we have lost the
world, do we begin to find ourselves.*
—Henry David Thoreau, *Walden* (1854)

Just before sunrise, the search-and-rescue captain quietly pulled me aside outside the earshot of my son and two sons-in-law. "We've had nine volunteers on the mountain all night with lights, whistles, and bullhorns," he said. "We've covered all nine trails beginning to end. There was no sign of her. At 4:00 a.m. we sent up a helicopter with FLIR thermography (forward-looking infrared radiometry), so we'll soon know where she is."

By dawn, the captain had his answer from the helicopter pilot: "No heat signature." Through a fog of fatigue and worry, I spotted my youngest son defying the rescue team and heading up the trail with a flashlight, hoping to succeed where the pros had failed. I knew I could not keep up with a determined, if ill-advised, thirty-two-year-old, so I stayed behind, asking the veteran search-and-rescue leader for his frank assessment.

"I don't want to alarm you, but I've been doing this a long time and it doesn't look good," he said. "I'm bringing in the dogs, so the best way for you to help is by bringing us some clothing your wife recently wore. Be back in an hour."

As I walked to my car to drive the twenty minutes from Millcreek Canyon to our home in Salt Lake City, I happened to overhear one exhausted, if indiscreet, rescuer refer to his canine replacements as "cadaver dogs."

Had Diana, my wife of nearly five decades, met with an accident—or worse? Had she fallen into a ravine? Did I need to worry about bears or mountain lions or coyotes?

Putting aside such images, I thought, *What will this mean to the lives of our children and grandchildren?* And, more selfishly, *How will the resolution of this long night change my own life?*

Returning to the immediacy of my highest-and-best-use clothes-gathering assignment, I refocused on making the drive from trailhead to valley. A bit irritated from the lack of sleep and a looming sense of dread, I wondered what in the world a sixty-five-year-old woman was doing hiking alone in the mountains.

In fact, she'd been preparing for a long-planned, week-long trek we were soon to take as a family. Diana was cramming, taking hikes on her own to get in shape, hoping to surprise all of us—me, her seven adult children, and their seven spouses—with her fitness. This hike, not far from our home in Salt Lake, was one in a series of increasingly challenging solo outings—yet one that was, on paper, easy enough that she felt no need to bring flashlights, whistles, warm clothing, survival gear, or maps. It was supposed to be a simple, safe hike—just four miles, albeit up steep terrain. She'd set out around three o'clock on Saturday and had expected to be home by 7:00 p.m. She wasn't.

As night fell and I'd begun to wonder where she was, I called our kids to see if they'd heard from their mother. None had. One daughter replied, however, that a few hours earlier she'd spotted a cell phone "pin" locating her on the peak of a nearby mountain. Apparently, Diana had been proud to reach the summit, so she'd dropped an electronic pin on it before her cell phone battery ran out.

It wasn't long before this clue led us to the trailhead that belonged to the pinned summit. Sure enough, Diana's locked car was sitting alone in the parking lot. Now, hours after nightfall, with no sign of her, a worried son-in-law called search and rescue and alerted the rest of the family. The long night's vigil had begun.

By now it was Sunday morning and I was alone, rummaging through our laundry room, looking for the clothing she'd worn prior to her hike. It had been cold overnight, and I found myself hoping Diana had taken a down jacket with her.

Once I'd gathered the clothing, I had twenty minutes to spare before heading back up the canyon for the arrival of the dogs. Since all of the news from the command center was turning grim, I was in no rush to get back to the mountain—indeed, I was beginning to give up hope and anticipate the grieving process.

As I walked around the house, I looked at photos of Diana and me together, and images of her with our children and grandchildren. I thought about what a happy and accomplished life she'd built. I also thought about the fast-moving rush of difficult tasks I'd face if the search-and-rescue mission failed, and whether there was anything I could do to get ahead of it. So, faced with some spare moments and hoping to find something productive to occupy my worried mind, I sat down at my computer to begin composing her obituary—just in case.

This may seem an odd, even macabre impulse. But strangely, this morbid exercise gave me a sense of calm, and became a level-setting pause in the long night's confusion. I found myself reflecting with a sense of wonder at how well Diana had lived her life. I thought about how well we'd complemented each other during our long marriage. Out of our early competitiveness, Diana's thriving instincts had gently defanged my striving ones. We'd developed a comfortable, life-enhancing harmony that gave each of us a far richer, more complex, and complete life than we'd have had making life's trek alone—or with a mate whose traits accentuated, rather than counterbalanced, our own. Sketching out my wife's obit required sober reflection, and within a few moments, the exercise had turned my dread into a moment of unexpected gratitude against this backdrop of imagining a worst-case scenario.

After a few minutes of this incongruous reflection, I loaded the car with her recently worn clothing. Driving into the mouth of the canyon, my reflections were abruptly interrupted by a call from search and rescue. Diana had turned up.

She had wandered into camp with a shattered wrist. She was exhausted, dehydrated, bruised, cut up, and cold—but very much alive. The ambulance took her to the hospital where she was cleaned up, warmed up, rehydrated, examined, and scheduled for surgery. Soon, a titanium plate with seven screws in her arm would serve as a lifelong reminder of her ordeal.

Eventually, I came to see this 2016 near-tragedy as a metaphor.

I've been an entrepreneur for forty-five years, and I've taught would-be entrepreneurs at Stanford Business School for a quarter century. In thinking about my business life in light of what had just happened in my personal one, it occurred to me that we send our students and young entrepreneurs into the business world with a general sense of needed provisions but little practical advice and very few complete maps—much as Diana left on her Saturday afternoon hike.

Just as Diana knew all about flashlights, trail mix, water bottles, walkie-talkies, the importance of hydration, of staying on trails, and of not hiking after dark or alone, in theory our students know about the perils of entrepreneurship and the requisite principles of effective leadership. But, like Diana—with the trail disappearing, discovering that she was ill-prepared, and trying to make it back to her car before nightfall—many students, full of knowledge, soon learn they don't have what they need when things don't go as planned. They are well prepared in theory but not in practice.

I teach at one of the world's great universities, so obviously I believe in the value of theory and book learning. At the same time, I'm convinced that leading people is often more a matter of EQ (emotional intelligence) than of IQ. And this most difficult of all business assignments—to serve as leader—is more a matter of attitude, of mind-set, and of maps than of the application of theories that only touch on elements of the leadership equation.

This book—the result of a lifetime of metaphorical treks in business and personal life—aims to provide readers with a manual for the kind of leadership that results in durable change. I've survived (and mostly enjoyed) at least three careers and a long marriage, and I've raised seven kids. I've held demanding roles, including CEO, CFO, chairman, lead director, adjunct professor, founder, author, entrepreneur, and investor.

During these endeavors, I've been lost more than once. I've relied on more than one rescuer. And I've occasionally had to turn back, to recalibrate, to reboot. But over time, I've learned how to better prepare and, more importantly, how to recover. I've learned what to do—and how to think—when things don't go as planned. I've figured out how to survive betrayal, miscalculation, and just plain bad luck. I've learned both how to live with disappointment and how to keep the occasional success from changing my values.

From these experiences, I've developed a framework—a set of principles, mind-sets, and self-talk—that may help others in their quests. Most focus on business, and this book is primarily a guide to leadership in that context. But the qualities that can help business leaders can also be quite useful in other contexts too: raising a family, leading a nonprofit, or even managing a classroom. Leadership comes in many forms, and—like any skill—it responds to principles, repetition, checklists, and feedback.

Though life can be messy and unpredictable, there are patterns and methods for increasing the odds of success—whether running a business or climbing a mountain. Through experience, I've developed considerable pattern recognition. I've "seen most movies" more than once and have a general sense for how they may end. My experience may help a few people get more of what they want out of life.

I'm writing this book for a specific kind of leader, the type I call an *entrepreneurial leader.* In contrast with pure entrepreneurs (who can launch things but can't necessarily run them at scale), presiders (who maintain the status quo but don't create durable change), managers (who simply make the trains run on time), administrators (who create and execute policies and procedures), and politicians (who compromise, rationalize, debate, and legislate), entrepreneurial leaders are able to launch something new, turn around a failing enterprise, and anticipate and make change before they have to. In an age of disruption, fickle consumers, fast-moving markets, and unprecedented social change, this type of nimble leadership is needed more than ever.

Anyone attempting life's biggest challenges—whether leading teams, companies, families, or just themselves—shouldn't venture out of base camp without a clear plan for action, organized into four categories:

1. Build Trust
2. Create a Mission
3. Secure a Team
4. Deliver Results

Building trust is table stakes—the necessary first step to legitimize the leader and give all stakeholders (not just employees) a reason to follow. *Creating a mission* is necessary because people can't do their best work without a sense of purpose. *Securing a team* allows leaders to leverage their own skills and put the best players on the field. *Delivering results* is the *sine qua non* of leadership: it's not only required, but it creates a flywheel-like momentum that yields more trust, a clearer mission, the ability to hire even better players.

I consider building trust, creating a mission, and securing a team as preparatory steps. Until you've done these things, there's little chance you'll be able to deliver anything. Trust, mission, and team can be enhanced by following a series of steps, which I outline in the first three sections of this book. Only with trust, mission, and team providing a firm base may a leader begin delivering on promises. Delivery requires confronting a dynamic but predictable set of circumstances. To deal with them, entrepreneurial leaders will benefit from a series of maps—and in the fourth section of this book, I provide the ones I find most useful.

I believe anyone can learn to do this. Too often, society idolizes once-in-a-generation charismatic leaders like Steve Jobs or Herb Kelleher. But one needn't be a natural-born leader. Anyone can develop these skills by following a systematic approach, cultivating the right mind-sets, asking the right questions, and applying the right principles and accumulated wisdom. Will taking this action enhance trust? Will it build on our mission? Will this help me attract a great team? And if we create this plan, can we actually execute on it? I've observed people change by using these maps, and I've seen organizations improve in dramatic and unanticipated ways. When led this way, people come together and make things happen.

The better one learns to follow this framework, the less perilous becomes the journey. Since these lessons are better learned through experience than through lecture, in the pages ahead I've tried to relate them by recounting stories—my own and those of colleagues at companies such as JetBlue, Bonobos, Trunk Club, Asurion, and other mostly business-to-business companies I've been fortunate enough to work with in my career.

This is not a manual for those merely seeking increased personal productivity, freedom from organizational constraints, or the perks and power of presiding. There are already plenty of manuals for how to pursue those things.

Instead, this book is aimed at those who hope to lead others, help them achieve their best, break new barriers, change the status quo, create a legacy, develop a brand, and enjoy a life-altering experience. In short, it's for people who aspire to "run stuff" in a manner that creates a durable, productive, pleasant, innovative, and flexible enterprise.

This is a manual for entrepreneurial leadership—the path that is a leader-manager's highest calling. It's the route I hope more people—in corporate life, nonprofit life, and civic and political life—will feel compelled to follow. Here's how.

THE WORLD NEEDS MORE ENTREPRENEURIAL LEADERS

The first responsibility of a leader is to define reality. The last is to say thank you. In between the two, the leader must become a servant and a debtor.
   —Max De Pree, *Leadership Is an Art*

I love many things about teaching at Stanford, but one of my favorite parts of the job is spotting people who have the ability to become entrepreneurial leaders—and watching the impact they can have on the world. Among my former students and colleagues, I have many such examples. Here's one of my favorites.

In 1994, not long after I began teaching at Stanford's Graduate School of Business, the young man working in the office next door asked to meet. His name was Kevin Taweel. Kevin had graduated from Stanford's MBA program two years earlier, and he'd opted to stick around as a case writer, working with professors to research and produce the cases that drive discussions in many classrooms.

At first, I thought Kevin needed advice about a case, but that wasn't it. In addition to writing cases, Kevin had raised $210,000 to fund his search for a small business he could buy. He'd located one, and he wanted to pitch me on investing.

His pitch didn't seem very compelling. Kevin and Jim Ellis, a recent student of mine, were planning to purchase a Texas-based company called Mr. Rescue. The company provided roadside assistance services, much like AAA has done for decades—if you get a flat tire, run out of gas, or need a tow, Mr. Rescue is there to help. On the surface, this didn't seem like a great growth business. Roadside assistance is a labor-intensive service industry that would be hard to scale, and having AAA as a competitor seemed like a pretty big obstacle to success.

I asked Kevin to let me think it over. The more I reflected, the more unimpressed I was with the basic business, the competitive landscape, and the growth potential. But I saw two compelling reasons to invest: Kevin and Jim. To my eyes, they were entrepreneurial leaders in embryo.

Before coming to Stanford, Kevin had played semipro soccer in Canada, and to me that said a lot about his ability to collaborate to work toward a goal. He'd earned a degree in mechanical engineering at McGill University and worked in mergers and acquisitions at Salomon Brothers. At Stanford, we'd worked on a case together, and I'd been impressed by his analytical skills and conscientiousness. His partner, Jim, had been a student in the first class I'd taught in the MBA program. There were fifty-six students in the group, and I'd given three of them a grade of H, meaning "honors." Jim was one of them.

So even though I wasn't enamored with the roadside repair business, I decided to write a check, in order to back Kevin and Jim.

They didn't disappoint. They lined up financing and paid $8.4 million to buy the company. They used the skills they'd learned at Stanford to grow it quickly, more than doubling its earnings before interest, taxes, depreciation, and amortization (EBITDA) in the first year. Soon they expanded, contracting with automotive, insurance, credit card, and wireless companies which could then offer roadside assistance services as add-ons to their clients. Then, as mobile phones took off in the late 1990s, they recognized that insuring cell phones was a similar—but far more attractive—business than roadside assistance, so they made a $7.6 million acquisition in that space. Within three years, they'd grown the company's revenues by more than tenfold.

Twenty-five years after my initial investment with them, Kevin still runs the company, now called Asurion.[1] (Jim left to pursue other opportunities in the early 2000s.) Today Asurion has 280 million customers in eighteen countries, to whom it offers tech support, extended warranties, and mobile technology protection plans. If you said yes to the insurance plan offered when you purchased your cell phone, you are likely an Asurion customer. Still privately held, Asurion generates more than $8 billion in annual revenue—not bad for a company whose initial business plan didn't seem very compelling.

Kevin Taweel is a great example of an entrepreneurial leader. As an executive, I've spent my career learning to be one, and I've spent twenty-seven years teaching students at Stanford to become agents of durable change. As an investor, I've learned to identify and back them; as a board member, I've tried to hire, develop, and promote them. As a leader, I've tried to learn from those further down the path. The aim of this book is to help you to pursue this journey, too, should you wish.

What do I mean by *entrepreneurial leader?*

Over many years of observing leaders and leading people myself, I have learned to recognize five distinct styles of leadership:

1. **The Presider**. From presiders we expect the preservation of values, the elegant representation of the team/company both within the enterprise and with its external constituencies, the efficient management of meetings, communications, and so on, and a sort of wise stewardship over the assets of the firm. Think of someone who spends his entire career at the same company and serves a relatively short stint as CEO—a time during which everything runs smoothly but nothing changes dramatically. He successfully presided.

2. **The Manager**. From managers we expect teams to be led to deliver on-time, on-budget, agreed-upon results. Managers are like conductors who understand the score and each instrument without having to play every one of them. Managers excel at

managing people, so they tend to focus on the team rather than the organization, its strategy, or its trajectory.

3. **The Administrator**. From administrators we expect the policies and processes that deliver predictability and efficiency. Administrators administrate process. They are disciplined and efficient but rarely creative or inspirational. They may successfully lead a bureaucracy or governmental entity, where rules and process guide day-to-day actions, but they may struggle to succeed in a dynamic or unpredictable environment.

4. **The Pure Entrepreneur**. From pure entrepreneurs we expect innovation, experiments, pilots, a future focus. Entrepreneurs excel at launching new things, but they often stumble when asked to lead a larger, steady-state business or turn around a faltering organization.

5. **The Politician**. From politicians we expect compromise and legislation that serve to rationalize decision making by others in charge of execution. They also understand and know how to use power. Political skill can be useful in many leadership contexts (particularly when in a highly democratic or collaborative culture), but overreliance on political skill rarely works well in a business setting.

Most leaders play most of these roles at some point in their careers. What sets entrepreneurial leaders apart is their ability to excel at all of these styles of leadership when necessary. In baseball, scouts talk about "five-tool players" who display excellent fielding, arm strength, foot speed, the ability to hit for average *and* hit for power. (One of the sport's ultimate five-tool players was Willie Mays, who was once my neighbor after he retired to California.) In a similar way, entrepreneurial leaders are five-tool businesspeople, capable of shifting easily between the styles and tasks of leadership, as the context and challenges demand.

Entrepreneurial leaders demonstrate a particular mind-set and an approach to problem-solving. They are change agents. They are intentional, staying true to their vision and agenda rather than only reacting to day-to-day turbulence. Over decades of trial and error, coaching and teaching, alternating between the arena and the academy, I've come to recognize the mind-sets, instincts, and maps that differentiate entrepreneurial leaders from other kinds of leaders.

The armed services have a reputation as a slow-moving bureaucracy, so it might seem an unlikely place for entrepreneurial leadership. But Stanley McChrystal defies that stereotype. I was privileged to meet McChrystal—the four-star general who'd led Joint Special Operations Command (JSOC) and overseen war efforts in Iraq and Afghanistan—in 2010, shortly after he'd retired from his military service, when we met to consider adding him to the board of directors at JetBlue.

Like everyone else, I was aware that McChrystal had resigned his post after a *Rolling Stone* article in which one of his direct reports was quoted making unflattering remarks about then vice president Joe Biden. (A Defense Department inspector general's investigation later cleared McChrystal of responsibility in this incident.) But I was also aware of the near-universal admiration for him among military and civilian leaders. As I conducted reference checks, I came across a quote from Defense Secretary Robert Gates describing McChrystal as "perhaps the finest warrior and leader of men in combat I have ever met."

Riding in a cab to the airport together after our first meeting, I asked McChrystal to describe how he led under the enormous stress of combat. Without hesitation, he responded that his definition of leadership is really quite simple: "It's not about me—it's about the mission."

A few years later, I read *Team of Teams*, McChrystal's account of how he'd turned the disparate branches of the US Special Forces into a cohesive unit. One metaphor especially appealed to me. McChrystal writes that, although history tends to depict leaders in heroic terms, he views the actual work of leading not as that of a hero, nor even as that of a strategy-savvy chess master, but instead as being very similar to the work of a "humble gardener."

Gardeners, McChrystal writes, succeed by doing the quiet, day-to-day maintenance that creates a nurturing environment in which plants can thrive. "Watering, weeding, and protecting plants from rabbits and disease are essential for success," he writes. "The gardener cannot actually 'grow' tomatoes, squash, or beans—she can only foster an environment in which the plants do so."[2] Over the last decade, I've had an opportunity to observe McChrystal in the boardroom, at his own consulting company, and during informal after-hours dinners. Although a skeptic might argue whether a career army officer can really have entrepreneurial instincts, to my mind, McChrystal epitomizes the ability to build trust, establish a mission, build a team, and execute to perfection. He's a role model for any aspiring entrepreneurial leader.

The same is true for Amy Errett, the founder and CEO of Madison Reed, the disruptive hair color company.[3] I first met Amy more than a decade ago, when she was an entrepreneur-in-residence at Maveron, the Seattle-based venture capital firm. She'd spent the previous five years successfully leading Olivia, a travel company focusing on the LGBT market. Maveron had asked me to come on as an advisor, and I spent a day in Seattle, observing and talking with the team. VC firms are partnerships, and Amy wasn't a partner, so on paper, she had little power. In meetings, she remained quiet—but when she spoke, her comments were incisive, and people listened. In particular, I remember the firm's discussions about a portfolio company that was faltering. It was clear to me the company needed to take radical action, but the partners were dithering. Amy spoke up: "You should just shut this down." Very quickly, Maveron grew to value her decisiveness and straight talk: they asked her to open a Maveron office in San Francisco, where she showed a knack for spotting nascent investments that could grow into substantial consumer brands.

In 2013, Amy left Maveron to start Madison Reed, which stood out from competitors' products by offering nontoxic hair products that gave women consistent results. As a leader at a start-up, Amy spent much of her time focusing on the company's culture. The entire company eats lunch together on Mondays, has regular social gatherings, and sponsors a collective Thanksgiving event at which team members share what they are grateful for. When the monthly employee survey results in a complaint, Amy reads it out loud to the team and invites a frank discussion. As one of the original investors in the company, I've been thrilled to watch Amy scale Madison Reed into a sizable, profitable consumer brand—but what most impresses me about Amy's unique skill set is her ability to shift back and forth from being an investor (during her years in venture capital) to an operating executive. Few people have the intellectual flexibility to do well in both spheres—and even fewer can create a cohesive team inspired by a common mission and led by principles. Her style is different from Stan McChrystal's—but she, too, is adept as an entrepreneurial leader.

It's not only new companies that benefit from having an entrepreneurial leader in the CEO role. For evidence of that, consider the career of Alan Mulally, who demonstrated extraordinary leadership prowess at companies that were founded in 1916 and 1903, respectively.

Mulally was born in Kansas, and as a teenager he was so inspired by the space race that he chose to study aeronautical aviation at the University of Kansas. Upon earning his master's degree in 1969, he took a job at Boeing, where he rose through a series of engineering jobs, leading development of the 777 airliner and eventually taking charge of Boeing's entire commercial aircraft business, which constituted the majority of its revenues. Mulally successfully led Boeing Commercial Airplanes through the post-9/11 recession, which hit the aviation industry especially hard. When Boeing purchased McDonnell-Douglas and Rockwell, Mulally led the integration to form the largest aerospace company in the world. In 2006, he became CEO of Ford Motor Company, which was then badly in need of a turnaround.

Mulally's accomplishments at Ford have become legendary. Coming into an insular, highly politicized atmosphere, he led with straight talk, an openness to ideas (even from low-level employees, whom he'd sit with in the cafeteria), and a courteous yet uncompromising accountability. "He came off like an overgrown Boy Scout, seasoning his conversations with words like *neat, cool,* and *abso-LUTE-ly*," writes biographer Bryce Hoffman in

American Icon: Alan Mulally and the Fight to Save Ford.[4] As he had at Boeing, Mulally required every senior executive to attend a Thursday morning meeting where they'd openly flag emerging business problems and work as a team to solve them. (This was in sharp contrast to the prior culture, which was dominated by covering up problems and pointing fingers when they were discovered.) Mulally worked to simplify Ford's product lineup and brand portfolio, while simultaneously shoring up its troubled finances before the Great Recession hit—a move that saved it from the bankruptcy filings of its competitors. In *American Icon*, Hoffman recalls Mulally as the epitome of a humble leader: one who favored a blue blazer and chinos over custom-made suits, who eschewed chauffeurs and instead drove Toyotas and Hondas during his commute (to better understand competitors' products), and whose strategy was simple enough for every hourly worker to understand.[5]

As with McChrystal, some might argue that since Mulally excelled as a leader at companies founded more than one hundred years ago, he can't possibly qualify as entrepreneurial. I disagree. Anyone who's tried to launch a new initiative, launch something completely new, or execute a true transformation within a very large company requires many of the same skills as someone founding a start-up. There is no doubt Mulally has the skills, instincts, and mind-set of an entrepreneurial leader.

Since retirement, Mulally has spoken several times in a class I teach at Stanford. In person, he's just as humble and self-effacing as the journalistic accounts have portrayed. My most vivid recollection of our time together was when he pulled two pieces of paper from a folder to show me. "This is the road map I used to lead at Boeing," he said, handing me a document with a simple list of diagrams and objectives. "And this is the road map I used to lead at Ford," he said, handing me a second document. I spent a minute comparing them closely. Then I realized the only difference was the name of the company at the top—otherwise, the road maps were exactly the same.

Mulally's road maps offer an important insight: once someone internalizes the skills and behaviors needed to be an entrepreneurial leader, they're highly portable. The context may change, but the skills of leadership do not.

The essentially transformative work of the entrepreneurial leader can be immensely fulfilling. The people you're leading will often appreciate what you do for them. External constituencies such as customers and investors may also have warm-and-fuzzy feelings for you. The days will be long, but when you go home each evening, you'll likely feel a sense of purpose and accomplishment.

To illustrate the value of this work, think for a moment how the world might have looked if Stanley McChrystal, Amy Errett, and Alan Mulally had not chosen to step into their leadership roles. Without McChrystal's work to transform the way Special Operations forces collaborate, the US war efforts in Afghanistan and Iraq would have been less successful, resulting in additional loss of life. Without Amy Errett's guidance, dozens of successful CEOs would have missed out on the mentoring she provided as a venture capitalist—and her current employees and customers at Madison Reed would have been left behind as well. And without Alan Mulally, Ford Motor Company might have been sold off for parts or mired in bankruptcy.

Their examples illustrate why entrepreneurial leaders are doing profoundly important and impactful work. Still, this demanding role is not for everyone. Being an entrepreneurial leader requires setting goals, developing strategies, staffing the execution, making assignments, and measuring results—all within the context of values that support a shared mission. By definition, an entrepreneurial leader can't control or micromanage the execution—but nonetheless, if the execution fails, he or she must be willing to take the heat.

Like the coach of a sports team or a team captain, succeeding in this role requires one to take a special joy in watching others reach summits. This kind of leadership is an act of stewardship—not a personal possession intended to glorify or enrich the position holder but an act of benevolence and self-sacrifice.

Some look at this array of challenges and ask themselves: Who needs it? Is it really worth complicating one's life with seemingly limitless responsibilities? No wonder many talented people choose to remain an individual contributor or the type of manager I call a presider—someone who excels at managing the day to day, and at preserving well-established institutions (and often enjoying the perks of leadership), but without any deep ambition to transform or transcend.

That's never true for an entrepreneurial leader. Their work is messy, largely intangible, and never-ending. Each day brings new problems and new decisions that present ambiguity and shades of gray.

Nonetheless, entrepreneurial leadership is the most impactful work any who would become a leader may do—and the world is made better by those who seek out its challenges.

BUILD
TRUST

Trust is base camp for preparing the entrepreneurial leader's attempt to lead a team to the summit. Trust animates the mission, is a predicate for recruiting a team, and enhances the interdependencies that deliver results. Without trust, companies can expect to experience political infighting, enterprise-damaging betrayals, and leadership crises. When trust is established, people come together, turnover declines, and once-transitory change becomes enduring. To move from presider, manager, administrator, pure entrepreneur, or politician to entrepreneurial leader, one must develop a high-trust personal brand.

STEP 1
ASSESSING CORE VALUES

The life which is unexamined is not worth living.
—Socrates, in Plato's *The Apology of Socrates*

In 1972, I was a student at Harvard Business School working toward an MBA. One afternoon I attended a guest lecture presented by the school's real estate club. The speaker was Trammell Crow, one of the country's most successful real estate developers. Although I had no way of realizing it at the time, choosing to attend this event would change the course of my life.

Trammell was born into a preacher's family in 1914 and grew up in East Dallas, Texas, the fifth of eight children. After serving in World War II, he passed the CPA exam and married Margaret Doggett, who came from a well-to-do family that owned a successful grain business. After a tragic auto accident took the lives of Margaret's parents, Trammell invested her inheritance in his first real estate project, a small warehouse. He never looked back.

Standing at that Harvard podium, Trammell talked about the principles he'd used to start and lead his firm, which designed, financed, built, and managed commercial real estate projects around the world. Midway through the hour, I found myself listening intently. While his sounded like an intriguing business, he seemed to me an even more interesting potential mentor, someone worth not just listening to for an hour but someone after whom I might model a business career.

The moment I remember most vividly in Trammell's talk came during the Q&A. One student asked what had accounted for his success. That's a prosaic question, and I expected Trammell to give a similarly clichéd answer—something along the lines of *hard work* or *finding passion*. Instead, he paused, scratched his bald head, and responded with a single, completely unexpected word: *love*.

He went on to describe, eloquently and authentically, how he loved what he did, the people who worked with him, and the clients for whom his firm built and managed properties. More than being profitable, he saw work as meaningful. What seemed to drive him was a deep sense of affection and caring for the people who worked with him (not *for* him) and the customers they worked for (not *sold to*). Only lately have psychologists begun to recognize the power of meaning when choosing a career; so at the time this was an insight I'd not expected.

Because people don't often talk about love and caring in MBA classrooms, the unusual discussion made a lasting impression on me. That evening, I went home and told my wife about Trammell Crow and his success-through-love philosophy of business. Diana listened to what I said, but more importantly, she took note of the look on my face and the sound of my voice as I spoke.

She responded, "You're going to go work with this Trammell Crow, aren't you?" I hadn't realized it at the time, but she was right.

After graduating, I took a job with Trammell's firm. Diana and I moved to Paris, where I began working with lenders, contractors, and prospective tenants, learning the business of commercial real estate. I performed well enough that a few years later, Trammell asked me to move to Dallas to become the firm's chief financial officer and, a few years after that, its CEO. In all, I spent eighteen years at Trammell Crow Company. During much of that time I worked in close proximity to the company's founder, sitting across from him in an open office.

From that vantage point, I learned what Trammell meant when he'd said his success was fueled by love. He was trusting and giving. He cultivated an abundance mentality—the sense that there is enough to go around for everyone, so one needn't be greedy. Even when the stakes were high, he conveyed a sense of lightheartedness and fun. When something went wrong he would respond with a shrug and a maxim: "There's another trolley every fifteen minutes." He exuded a confidence and optimism that went beyond the circumstances of the moment.

Psychologists differentiate between personality and character. Personality is easily observed by appearance and behavior. If you spend thirty minutes interviewing someone for a job or even on a first date, you can get a sense of his or her personality. But personality is superficial, and it is easier to change than character. We all know people whose personality adapts to their surroundings, who behave one way at work, another with old friends, and another at church on Sunday.

Character, on the other hand, runs deep: it's typically defined as the mental and moral qualities that make a person distinctive. Character is formed over time and is a function of our fundamental values—the things we hold dear. The reason many spend years dating before proposing is to assess a potential partner's character—something that can't be done in a few dates.

Over years of watching Trammell, I began to recognize that these qualities—love, generosity, confidence, optimism, and trust—represented his core values, which made up the most essential elements of his character. These core values were the reason I chose to go to work for him, and ultimately came to trust him. These core values were a vital part of what made him an effective leader.

Unwavering values allows one to behave predictably, which is a requisite for building trust. Therefore, aspiring entrepreneurial leaders should conduct a deep and introspective inventory of their core values, affirming the ones that will help them as leaders and seeking to temper the ones that will be counterproductive.

Core values are not immutable, like eye color or height, but they are deep-seated and resistant to change. Values are typically formed during childhood. In nearly everyone, parents play a pivotal role. Therefore, it's unusual to find someone whose values change dramatically once they are far along into adulthood. And when it does happen, it's often the result of a tragedy, a near-death experience, or other epiphany. Unlike one's *operating system* (discussed in the next chapter), values are not habits of mind that can be easily modified.

This self-analysis and introspection can be an important part of the journey toward entrepreneurial leadership. In business school, nearly every student takes some form of the Myers-Briggs assessment, which delivers a sense of whether the person is an introvert or extrovert and relies on thinking or feeling, sensing or intuition, perception or judgment. Aspiring MBAs value this information because self-knowledge about the way one navigates the world becomes especially important as people move into leadership roles. Others participate in talk therapy, read self-help books, or write journals to better understand their own values and from where they originate.

As one grows older, it often becomes easier to recognize a value in oneself and trace it back to its origins. Let me use an example from my own life in which I discovered a self-centeredness that I knew I'd need to change.

In middle school, I was an outgoing adolescent, but when our class put on a school play, I was assigned a peripheral, nonspeaking role. All I remember is that my assignment was to stand near the edge of the stage wearing a heavy winter coat and stay silent while the principal actors delivered lines at center stage.

On the night of the performance, with my parents in the audience, I grew a bit bored with my insignificance to the plot. So I started hamming it up—dramatically wiping sweat from my brow and miming how I was too hot in this heavy coat. The audience noticed my antics and laughed. The episode lasted just a couple of seconds, and I didn't think much of it—until after the play ended. My parents were upset that I'd been upstaging the other actors and drawing unnecessary attention to myself. Naturally, they admonished me to be less vain and self-centered.

I'm sure my parents thought little of the incident after that evening. But I thought a lot about it. As a result, I learned to avoid putting myself in the spotlight. Instead, I began striving to redirect the spotlight to others. In attempting to change, I began to deflect rather than to seek attention. Instead of self-centered, I tried to become other-centered.

Sixty years after that school play, my rocky introduction to humility has developed into an appreciation of humility as a core value—and much of it I trace to this memorable interaction with my parents. Fortunately, I learned to expand on this limited notion of humility to include learning from my mistakes, embracing feedback, and generally feeling awe and a sense of gratitude.

In my case, this minor intervention from my parents has proven useful. Jim Collins, the former Stanford adjunct professor whose books include *Built to Last* and *Good to Great*, has identified humility as a defining quality of the people he deems "Level 5 leaders." He believes this finding is counterintuitive, since so many business leaders (think of Lee Iacocca or Mark Cuban) intentionally put themselves in the spotlight. Collins writes: "A Level 5 leader is an individual who blends extreme humility with intense professional will. According to our five-year research study, executives who possess this paradoxical combination of traits are catalysts for the statistically rare event of transforming a good company into a great one."[1]

Beyond humility, what other values do I most often see in successful entrepreneurial leaders—the kind who inspire trust *from* and demonstrate trust *in* colleagues and subordinates? Let me highlight three.

Running toward the Fire: When a bomb went off near the finish line of the Boston Marathon in 2013, most of the nearby spectators instinctively began running away from the blast and resulting devastation. But US Army colonel Everett Spain—at the time, a Harvard Business School student—ran toward the explosion, into the smoke, to try to help the victims. "I can say with perfect honesty that it was not me who ran toward the smoke," he later explained, "but the values deliberately imprinted on me by my faith, my family, my friends, my mentors, the many character-building institutions I've been privileged to be associated with, and our American spirit."[2]

Likewise, when a terrorist on a French train began firing an AK-47 during the summer of 2015, Alek Skarlotos (a specialist in the Oregon National Guard) and Spencer Stone (an airman in the US Air Force), and a civilian named Anthony Sadler similarly ran toward the gunfire, overpowering and subduing the gunman.[3]

In my Stanford classes, I can often spot students who are returning to school after a stint in the military. The experience is evident in their posture, their organization, the respect with which they address others, and the general crispness and discipline with which they carry themselves. Anyone who's completed military service will recognize it as a formative, values-enhancing experience—and even those of us who haven't may quickly recognize it in others.

But one needn't have military experience to learn to *run toward the fire*—to proactively and aggressively attack problems, which in business only rarely involves life-threatening consequences. Indeed, wherever they learned this value, most of the entrepreneurial leaders I know have this same disposition—to run toward problems.

Integrity: Entrepreneurial leaders are also often distinguished by a second core value: a deep sense of integrity. *Integrity* is a word with multiple definitions, and most people tend to associate it with honesty, moral behavior, and a tendency to follow rules. These are virtues, no doubt, but in assessing entrepreneurial leaders, I've learned to focus on the second definition: to be whole and undivided, the way an engineer might speak of the structural integrity of a building.

Having the core values included in this second version of integrity means behaving in predictable ways, regardless of the setting. And as others come to trust how you'll respond, you've empowered them. They'll have confidence to take actions on their own. They'll act as they believe you would, confident there'll be no incriminations or second-guessing.

By empowering them, you'll have increased the power of the organization to move quickly, confidently, and durably. Indeed, a chief characteristic of the entrepreneurial leader is that he or she creates change that is durable precisely because of the others who have been recruited, sure of the predictability of the team and of the internal consistency of the leader.

Perseverance: The third core value I observe most frequently in successful entrepreneurial leaders is the willingness to persevere—the characteristic Collins describes above as "intense professional will." Many of the people I meet in whom this core value is evident developed it in one of three places: participation in youth sports, doing the unpleasant manual labor of summer jobs, or mastering a musical instrument.

Becoming good at a sport is difficult. Coaches ask you to do more than you think is possible. Many days you don't want to go to practice. During some seasons, your team will lose more than it wins. In team sports, you will need to work with others to be successful. But in any sport, you will need to learn the value of perseverance—to keep going when you would prefer to quit, to continue to seek success even when it seems unlikely, and to choose a path that is hard instead of one that is easy.

Likewise, teenagers' summer jobs can be formative experiences. Bussing tables, shingling a roof, thinning sugar beets—these tasks are dirty, hot, boring, and repetitive (I've done them all). You work hard over long days for relatively low pay. (When I bussed tables, I earned seventy-five cents an hour.) Billions of people around the globe continue to work like this, and even if you become someone who sits in a comfortable office using your mind instead of your hands, there's a good chance many people lower in the organization—people who are essential to your organization—are doing sweaty, uncomfortable, or even physically risky tasks. There's value in having spent time doing this: you learn to do hard and uncomfortable things and develop empathy for people who spend their professional lives in this manner.

Finally, learning to play an instrument requires hours of practice and precision. As my wife often reminded our children when they were learning to play the piano, there is no cramming for a musical performance. You simply have to put in the hours to gain proficiency.

After taking an objective look at who we are and how we came to be that way, careful introspection will yield an assessment of the forces that guide our actions—our core values. This is a vital analytical step to becoming an entrepreneurial leader. There are two reasons this is critical. First, the process of introspection will invariably reveal less desirable qualities among our existing core values—whether a hot temper, self-absorption, lack of empathy, or fondness for status or power. These will get in the way of others trusting us. Only when seen for what they are can these undesirable tendencies be addressed. An understanding of our limitations, foibles, and weaknesses is a necessary step to becoming a leader who can be trusted and whose legacy will be one of durable change.

And secondly, since successful entrepreneurial leaders are generally humble, proactive, predictable, and perseverant, recognizing these as core values to cultivate will be the first step in finding one's North Star for developing a deep-seated, reliable trust.

Since trust is the most powerful currency of the entrepreneurial leader, and since creating durable change is almost impossible in a low-trust environment, entrepreneurial leaders must be able to convince others that they can rely on a leader's ability to learn (humility), willingness to take measured risks (proactivity), and integrity and commitment to overcome (perseverance). Indeed, turnarounds—a predictable element of many entrepreneurial journeys—only succeed when lenders, investors, suppliers, *and* customers trust that an entrepreneurial leader is not merely an entrepreneur lighting fires, a presider maintaining the status quo, a politician playing to various constituencies, or a manager-administrator running things well.

All who are party to the entrepreneurial journey must trust that the entrepreneurial leader is committed to learning from the marketplace (humility), has the energy to pilot change and to sunset what isn't working (proactivity), and the stamina to overcome obstacles and survive challenges (perseverance).

RECAP

▶ Identify your core values by making a clear-eyed assessment of where you spend your time, money, and mind share. Then decide if your values are getting in the way of your effectiveness.

▶ Evaluate how you might increase your tendency to (1) run toward the fire, (2) display a version of integrity that aligns actions with utterance, and (3) demonstrate dogged persistence.

▶ Take on hard work and service to others without obvious remuneration to better appreciate the plight of others you may be called upon to lead.

STEP 2

REWRITING YOUR OPERATING SYSTEM

Everyone has the power to say, This I am today. That I shall be tomorrow.

—Louis L'Amour, *The Walking Drum* (1984)

When I was an MBA student, I met many people whose backgrounds and aspirations were different from mine. One classmate who stands out in my memory was a young man from Long Island living across the hallway from me. His name was Ray Dalio.

Ray was a good student, but his real passion wasn't for management—it was for investing. Back then, Ray was obsessed with a practice known as technical trading, in which investors focus exclusively on finding patterns in the company's daily stock price movements. In contrast with traditional investors, who look at balance sheets and income statements, technical traders obsess over these patterns, believing they will predict when the stock is set to rise or fall.

This all looked like utter madness to me, a silly game on par with palm reading or astrology. As we approached graduation and I pondered my classmates' futures, I was concerned about how Ray and his piles of mysterious stock charts were going to fare. Honestly, I wondered how he was going to make a living.

Today Ray Dalio is worth $18.1 billion and is the twenty-fifth richest person on the planet, according to Forbes. Bridgewater Associates, the firm he launched after we graduated, is the most successful hedge fund investment company in the industry's history. Where I saw madness, Ray clearly had a method.

In 2017, Ray set out to describe his method in a book he called, very simply, *Principles*. The book describes Ray's attempt to *systematize* the process of management. He writes: "Great managers are not philosophers, entertainers, doers, or artists. They are engineers. They see their organizations as machines and work assiduously to maintain and improve them. They create process-flow diagrams to show how the machine works and evaluate its design. . . . They don't do this randomly. They do it systematically, always keeping the cause-and-effect relationships in mind."[1]

Next to knowing one's core values, the most important attribute an entrepreneurial leader can possess is a predictable, reliable, and intentional personal operating system. If that operating system isn't yet as reliable as the leader wants, refining it to that point should be a priority.

Everybody knows what a computer's operating system is. It helps process the information the computer takes in, sets rules and priorities, and brings an orderliness to how the computer approaches its work. Humans have personal operating systems too. An entrepreneurial leader must translate priorities into actions in order to generate results. This begins at the interface between brain and heart—in the "applications" used to solve problems and make decisions. In the same way that an operating system guides a computer's operations, a leader's personal operating system guides his or her everyday actions.

Ray Dalio has succeeded because he's created a firm with elaborate systems, flow-charts, and processes that guide its everyday decisions. Together, they are the firm's operating system. But before a leader can create an organization that functions this way, he or she must refine his or her personal operating system—the habits he or she uses to lead—and learn to act systematically in everyday practice.

Whether genetically or socially determined, set in motion by parents, nurtured by peers, or simply welling up as inchoate emotion, most of us think we inherited how we react to stimuli, how we process information, and, especially, how we feel. By adulthood, many people stop thinking about it. It feels ingrained and foundational. We simply react. "After all," we say to ourselves, "that's just how I am."

This is a mistake. Reactions are not purely derivative of upbringing or DNA. They are, instead, choices. You can control them. And like a programmer, you can rewrite and repair your own operating system so that it represents your best self and makes you the predictable, reliable leader that people will want to follow. Indeed, to craft your approach to that of a leader who may lead durable change, you must.

Anson Dorrance, coach of the University of North Carolina women's soccer team, has led his athletes to twenty-three NCAA championships. He writes: "Deliberate actions, ordinary in themselves, performed consistently and carefully, made into habits; [and] compounded together, added up over time yield excellence." He asserts that new habits are within the reach of everyone, as he challenges young women to raise their sights and change their behavior.[2]

Stephen Covey, writing in *The 7 Habits of Highly Effective People*, puts it another way. He emphasizes the importance of people recognizing the truth in the statement "I am what I am today because of the choices I made yesterday"—and that in recognizing this, they realize that if they make different choices today, they will be different people tomorrow.[3]

I have personal experience with making difficult changes. As a young leader, when I undertook an effort to rewrite my operating system, I began with three mantras—sometimes repeating them several times a day in an effort consciously to override my natural instincts: *It's not about me. I am not my emotions. I have all I need.*

1. **"It's not about me."** Like many younger people, I tended to put myself at the center of a self-referencing universe. Once I discovered that most people interpret the world only as it

affects them, I realized that no one was paying much attention to how *I* came across because they were so caught up in how *they* came across. This realization liberated an other-centered focus and, with it, the habit of listening without agenda. I began setting aside my arguments, ignoring what I might say next, and putting on hold any evaluation of what I was hearing. Instead, I began listening simply to see how well I could summarize the thoughts of another—to capture and organize the essence of another's point of view better than they had articulated it. Soon, by adding empathy and patience, the discipline of *removing* myself from the center allowed me to better formulate my own thoughts—and, ultimately, to thrive at the center.

2. **"I am not my emotions."** Most of us feel emotions welling up as if they have a will of their own. Defendants who describe crimes of passion betray this logical leap, as if emotions are irrepressible and ungovernable. Good managers, however, train themselves to rein in emotions. I've concluded that my best decisions have been the product of analysis *plus* instinct. I consider my instincts, because I recognize the possibility that my heart knows things my head doesn't, but I avoid overreliance on instinct.

3. **"I have all I need."** No one likes failing. But in any large or meaningful project, missteps are inevitable. When failures happen, many people harbor a tendency to blame others, or bad luck, or lack of resources—anything but themselves. When I was young, I sometimes fell into this trap. Over time, I recognized I had no reason to lay off my failures on others. I had what I needed to get the job done, and if I didn't, it was on me. It reminded me to move beyond my failures and limitations. Soon I came to embrace the notions that there's information in failure and that defeat can serve as preamble to victory. "I have all I need" reminds me that failure is often fleeting and

temporary. This led me to develop a calm assurance that I have what I need to do whatever lies before me.

Eventually, these early attempts at self-talk began to stick. I began to adopt these three new attitudes as if they were natural. I found myself feeling (and acting) less selfish or self-centered, angry, defensive, or anxious. As I internalized the mantras, I thought about them less often. New patterns took over, and new habits took root. My operating system was being slowly rewritten, and as that happened, I was becoming a more reliable and more effective leader.

My own set of mantras are idiosyncratic, based on the specific deficiencies in my personal operating system that caused me to struggle. Everyone's attempts at self-correction will be different. The point is to identify what needs fixing and begin to fix it.

Any attempt to repair or improve one's own operating system must begin with an honest appraisal of flaws, imperfections, and negative tendencies. Sometimes we recognize these flaws by simple reflection. Very often, we recognize our imperfections in the pattern of feedback we receive from others. In other instances, we recognize our less-than-ideal habits by watching role models and then emulating them. In some cases, executive coaches or therapists can provide a helpful outside view and a path of guidance toward change.

During my long career, I've continually been impressed by people I have had the chance to observe as they engaged in the hard work of rewriting their personal operating systems.

One example is Andrew Saltoun, a former student of mine at Stanford. After graduating with his MBA in 2008, Andrew launched a search fund and set out to find a small company he could buy, run, and grow. Prior to entering Stanford, Andrew had worked on Wall Street, where he refined an investor's mind-set—a binary, go/no go orientation. This makes sense, since the biggest decision investors make is whether to invest or not invest. Sure enough, during the beginning months of his search, Andrew began to recognize that the habits and worldview he'd developed during his years working in investment banking and private equity might not be optimal for someone who would be running a small business.

Here's how Andrew describes the different mind-set he decided to cultivate: "Let's say I created a financial model back in my investment banker days. I'd take the top line and set it to grow at a certain rate and add a point or two to margins over time. Today, my worldview is 'Okay, that sounds great, but now tell me: Exactly *how* are you going to achieve that revenue growth? Where are the new customers coming from? Why are margins improving?'"[4] Instead of making straight-line assumptions, the way traders and bankers often do, today Andrew thinks like an operator—focusing on the levers he will push, the goals he will set, the way he will motivate his team, and the milestones they must reach to actually achieve growth.

"For me, this was a really intentional shift—a redefinition of my mentality,"[5] Andrew says, describing it as an important element of a larger evolution he pursued, from being an individual contributor to a manager to a leader. To achieve this transformation, he read voraciously, listened to podcasts, hired executive coaches, and constantly asked for feedback from board members and investors (who included me).

Andrew's journey required patience: he launched his search for a business just a few weeks before Lehman Brothers cratered and the financial crisis ensued—not an ideal time to buy a private company. It took nearly three years until he purchased Integra Partners, a company that creates a platform between health insurers, patients, and medical equipment suppliers. As Integra's CEO, Andrew used his new mind-set to quickly drive growth: in less than four years, he grew the head count from thirteen to more than 150 and revenue from $29 million to approximately $125 million. When he sold the company to Tufts Health Plan in 2015, investors recouped more than eleven times the money they'd put into the deal. Today Andrew continues to serve as Integra's CEO, but he also invests his money in other entrepreneurs—and when he does, he encourages them to engage in a focused and intentional effort to rewrite their own operating systems.

Another entrepreneurial leader I've observed who has developed her own operating system is Bonny Simi, who may have the most unusual résumé of anyone I know. Bonny attended Stanford as an undergrad in the 1980s, where it took her seven years to graduate because she was simultaneously training and competing as a member of the US Olympic luge team. After graduating, Bonny took a job as an on-camera television reporter for a large San Francisco station, while still competing in the luge and taking weekend lessons to get her private pilot's license. Over time, Bonny realized she enjoyed flying more than broadcasting, so she shifted her ambitions and became a pilot at United Airlines, eventually serving in that role for thirteen years. (During that stretch, she was promoted to left-seat captain.) In the early 2000s, she moved to JetBlue, where she continued flying a couple of times a month while moving to an executive track. At one point, she ran all of JetBlue's talent operations; today, she serves as president of JetBlue Technology Ventures, a Silicon Valley-based operation that invests in startups related to the airline business.

Identifying and mentoring high-potential entrepreneurs, which Bonny now does most days, is completely different from flying a hundred-seat Embraer 190 aircraft. So Bonny has refined her operating system to allow her to move from highly regimented and focused work to highly creative work, as if she has two fundamental operating systems upon which she can call. "Everyone has a left brain and a right brain," she says. "Your left brain is very structured, and your right brain is very creative. When I'm serving as a pilot, I rely on my left brain. You don't want an innovative pilot who is creative—you want someone who's following standard operating procedure, doing it the same way every time."[6] To prepare for this mental shift, Bonny regularly reviews manuals and checklists the day before she flies, like all pilots, so as to go into the high-focused, uninterruptable mode she requires when in command of an aircraft.

At the same time, she recognizes that there are elements of the pilot's job that help her be empathetic with the entrepreneurs she works with at her day job. "A pilot wears a lot of hats," she says. "You're sort of the mayor of this little city of a hundred people in the sky for two hours, not unlike what an entrepreneurial leader must do. If there's a problem while airborne, you can't pull over and park to work the problem—you have to manage it in real time by utilizing all the resources you have at hand."[7]

Successful entrepreneurial leaders learn to make these mental shifts as part of their operating system. They may require a different mind-set when talking to a potential investor, a potential employee, or a potential customer. Even if they are introverted, they know there are times at which they will need to emphasize their gregarious side, grit their teeth, and work the room. As Bonny puts it, "It's almost like you have two different personalities."[8]

Most leadership journeys start modestly. When a team is made up of fewer than a half-dozen people, a new leader's job may be simply to serve as domain expert with assistants to carry some of the load. In this role, the fledgling leader may work as a sort of supercharged performer, an enhanced doer, an incipient manager—but not yet a full-fledged leader.

Initially, the transition from producer to manager is about dealing with increased complexity—about keeping more balls in the air, about taking responsibility for the work of others, about intervening with discretion, and about managing tasks that are part of a strategic whole.

Later, as management turns into leadership, the leader's job description changes. To create durable institutional change, the entrepreneurial leader must learn to adapt and help others to do that too.

This self-knowledge is the foundation for a level of trust that starts with deep reflection and with self-talk and turns into an ability to deliver on compelling objectives, staff the execution, remove obstacles, and help team members to the summit. We become what we think about. Decide what you want to be, design your personal brand, and repair the operating system you inherited.

From this and other journeys into leadership, I've concluded that *self-management*—the starting point for leading others—emanates from a code deep within that can be "cracked" with self-talk. By borrowing different lenses through which to see events and studying the best practices of the best leaders, one can modify one's operating system until change becomes permanent.

Even in my seventies, I continue to refine my personal operating system. More than a century after Frederick Taylor held stop watches over factory workers to try to find ways they could do their tasks faster, the never-ending quest for improvement—first in oneself and only then in others—remains the essence of good management—a part of the skill set the entrepreneurial leader will need to master.

RECAP

▶ Recognize that you are the "master of your fate, the captain of your soul" (read "Invictus" by William Ernest Henley) and are capable of developing the operating system you want to have.

▶ Create three mantras that address the obstacles most in the way of your effectiveness, then repeat them as you harvest feedback until they become a natural response.

▶ Realize you will need different operating systems for different tasks as you move from manager to leader. Be flexible and patient with yourself as you try on different lenses.

STEP 3

ESTABLISHING YOUR PERSONAL BRAND

Behavior is a mirror in which everyone shows his image.
—Goethe, *Maxims and Reflections* (1833)

I n 2007, I became the first investor in a company called Bonobos, founded by two Stanford MBA students, Brian Spaly and Andy Dunn. Bonobos, which I will discuss further in several other sections of this book, aimed to reinvent the way men bought pants, utilizing a unique, superior-fitting design Brian had painstakingly created. Their plan, quite a new idea at the time, was to sell over the Internet.

By 2009, the company was starting to gain some traction—but the founders were no longer seeing eye to eye. Their deep friendship had been undermined by a series of disagreements about the business. The situation, as Andy recalled in an interview with podcast host Guy Raz, was compounded by his own clinical depression. After a stalemate in which the two founders would coexist at work but barely speak, Andy pulled Brian aside on a quiet Saturday and made a radical suggestion. "I just asked him, 'Hey, would you be willing to step aside, given everything that's going on?' He got a little teary, and he looked and he said 'Yeah,'" Andy recalls. "He was just unbelievably dignified about the whole thing."[1]

Not long afterward, Brian made an appointment to see me. After leaving Bonobos, he'd been asked to become CEO of a still-tiny start-up that was also in the men's fashion space. It was called Trunk Club. The company offered a service in which stylists would consult with customers by video chat, then send them a box of hand-picked clothing. Customers could try items on at home, purchase what they wanted, and return what they didn't. Brian had been meeting with potential investors. But his departure from Bonobos had raised questions that made them unwilling to write a check.

I'm not exactly a clotheshorse, so I'd never heard of Trunk Club. I had no idea how big a market there'd be for a service this like. But when Brian asked me to consider making an investment and offered to send me detailed information and projections, I told him not to bother. I didn't need to see the business plan. He could count on me as an investor, simply because I knew and respected his personal character and reputation. I made the investment not based on an analysis of market size, pricing power, or execution risk. I made it because of Brian's personal brand, because of how well I'd seen him operate during Bonobos's early days, and because of the elegance and grace with which he'd opted to leave that company. Regardless of the underlying idea, Brian is someone I wanted to be in business with. He had earned my trust.

(As a postscript, my decision to rely on Brian's reputation worked out well for both Brian and me: in 2014, he sold Trunk Club to Nordstrom for more than $300 million.)

Reputations are sticky. Positive or negative, everyone has one. They accumulate slowly over time, and they do so whether you try to actively manage what others think of you or not.

In our professional lives, our reputations are often called our personal brands—meaning what people who know us think and say about us when our name comes up. When we check references as part of the hiring process, we are assessing and auditing the candidate's personal brand.

Tom Peters, the former McKinsey consultant who catapulted to fame when he coauthored *In Search of Excellence* in the early 1980s, popularized the concept of personal branding in "The Brand Called You," a 1997 cover story in *Fast Company*.[2] Although the concept of professional reputation had been around for centuries before Peters wrote about it, he perceptively identified a series of trends that was beginning to make it more important.

More professionals were freelancing, moving between companies, and working with people outside their own firm more frequently; these actions increased the circle of coworkers who had firsthand knowledge of how someone performed at work. Email was reducing the gate-keeping power of administrative assistants (who previously screened phone calls), giving people an easier way to connect with one another based on reputation. The most important trend: many more professionals, even those employed at big companies, were spending much more time working on discrete projects, which present opportunities to show off skills in a way that the less-visible, day-to-day tasks of management sometimes don't.

"Regardless of age, regardless of position, regardless of the business we happen to be in, all of us need to understand the importance of branding," Peters wrote. "We are CEOs of our own companies: Me Inc. To be in business today, our most important job is to be head marketer for a brand called You."[3]

More than two decades later, much of Peters's wisdom still holds. At the same time, based on the behaviors displayed by my students at Stanford, there are at least two big misconceptions about personal branding.

The first is that one's personal brand is mostly created via social media, and that its strength can be quantified by the number of one's followers or connections on Twitter or LinkedIn. By contrast, consider companies with strong brands: Mercedes-Benz, Five Guys, or JetBlue. When I say the name, do you have a vivid sense of what each of these companies stands for, what each is promising consumers, and how much faith you can have in their ability to deliver on that promise? Now stop and consider: Do you follow *any* of the three on Twitter? (I'm guessing no.) In fact, these brands have been built not on social media but on their everyday interactions with consumers through years of delivering on what people expect from them.

Social media can be a useful tool in establishing "weak ties" to people you may want to meet, to keep in touch with existing contacts, and to share useful information. In isolated instances (such as an Instagram fitness model), it may be the primary method one has used to build a brand. But for most of us, relying primarily on social media to build a personal brand remains the exception, not the rule. Your personal brand is not a function of your last five tweets. Just as with a product or a corporate brand, a personal brand is established over years of work and is based on others' repeated assessments of your behavior and integrity.

The second misconception is that the best way to build your personal brand is to engage in self-promotional behavior—to brag, show off, and advertise your own successes. People generally react negatively to self-promoters, the same way they react to over-aggressive, inauthentic networkers. Even though many companies have built brands through mass-market advertising, and even as we spend more of our lives on social media, I continue to believe that the strongest personal brands are built differently, via one-to-one, in-real-life interaction—that is, the things we do with and for each other. We build our brands a conversation at a time, an action at a time, and a decision at a time.

My view of how to build one's personal brand is consistent with the work of Wharton psychologist Adam Grant, which he describes in his book *Give and Take*. As his title suggests, he divides the world into givers and takers based on this divide over generosity and reciprocity. He explains: "Takers have a distinctive signature: they like to get more than they give. They tilt reciprocity in their own favor, putting their own interests ahead of others' needs. Takers believe that the world is a competitive, dog-eat-dog place. They feel that to succeed, they need to be better than others. To prove their competence, they self-promote and make sure they get plenty of credit for their efforts."[4]

No surprise: I aspire to live in the giver lane. Grant describes givers' worldview this way: "They tilt reciprocity in the other direction, preferring to give more than they get. . . . [Givers] help others without expecting anything in return. If you're a giver at work, you simply strive to be generous in sharing your time, energy, knowledge, skills, ideas, and con-nections with other people who can benefit from them."[5]

People who consistently behave as givers tend to have strong and authentic personal brands. The people in their networks have real relationships with them—ones based not simply on having clicked the "follow" button after seeing something clever online. As you seek to build your personal brand, avoid the temptation to overinvest in social media, or to use it as a measuring stick. And avoid behaving like a braggart. Instead, aim for a quieter and more authentic consistency, reliability, and generosity.

Personal brands share at least one similarity with corporate brands: it's easier to build a positive brand from a blank slate than it is to turn around a brand that's developed negative baggage. As with commercial brands, a person's core attributes will tend to be self-reinforcing and hard to modify. This is why it's important to consider rewriting your operating system sooner than later, in order to elevate desired brand attributes to the top of the list of the changes you're making. Young people can shorten the time it takes to build a brand if they start early, are intentional, and habituate the behaviors that are consistent with the brand they aspire to embody.

And although personal brands are sticky, they are simultaneously fragile—particularly brand attributes that involve dimensions of integrity. You know what people say about brand and reputation: "It takes twenty years to build a brand and five minutes to ruin it."

Task number one in brand-building is to select attributes consistent with a unique value proposition. For example, not every car company can be—or wants to be—Mercedes-Benz. Indeed, by numbers, more customers buy Toyotas than Mercedes (partly because of the expense). What customers want is a brand they can trust to keep its promises with respect to their decision criteria.

In building a brand that will serve as a foundation for trust, start not with what *you* want but what your customer wants. Who will be your likely customers? Where are the gaps in the market? What are competitors not providing? What are the half-dozen promises they can trust you to deliver?

Then, as you think about the attributes you want to emphasize, think about the kinds of core values you have deep inside you (as discussed in Step 1) and the operating system that governs your day-to-day behaviors (as discussed in Step 2.) If you aim to be known for creativity, seek out projects that will require you to demonstrate it. Entrepreneurial leaders tailor brand attributes to the target market, whether they are dealing with a product or themselves. As leader, you can accelerate the market-sorting mechanism by being (a) intentional about what you stand for, (b) accurate and persuasive in how you describe it, and (c) relentless in its delivery.

For example, working on my first turnaround experience, as CFO of Trammell Crow in the late 1970s, I decided I wanted personally to emerge with a reliable, predictable brand—one anyone could "take to the bank." Looking back, I realize that a determination to be trustworthy was derivative of having to give lenders the disappointing news that we could not repay them as we reworked debt and laid people off. Sugarcoating the situation wouldn't have helped. By dealing with all parties candidly and transparently, I worked to establish trust—in our relationship, on behalf of the company, and as a person. When I think about my personal brand, I realize that I seek high trust as a core attribute—and this episode provided an opportunity to demonstrate that to others.

To get a good sense of the current state of your personal brand, ask five people who know you best to describe you using just a few adjectives. Look for overlap in what you hear. If you've asked the right people, you may not like everything they tell you. This is good news. It means you're getting useful feedback on what you might do to rewrite your operating system. After listening to and reflecting on this feedback, create an intentional plan for the brand attributes you want to emphasize, to subtly reposition how others see you—based not on spin, but on behavior.

One of my favorite conversations about the subtle shadings of a personal brand came in my role as a father. My youngest daughter was applying to college. One application question asked her to list the five adjectives that best described her. Within the family, she had a reputation for being determined, even stubborn. We talked about alternative ways to describe this: dutiful, reliable, hard-charging, or persistent. The essence of her brand—as with most brands—was in the nuance. By examining the subtleties against the mirror of her behavior, we worked to refine the brand that others have come to trust.

Sometimes personal brands can extend and expand in ways you don't expect. Arianna Huffington is a great example of that. During the 1990s and early 2000s, Arianna established a brand as a thoughtful writer and political commentator. She was a frequent presence on CNN, and her website the *Huffington Post* had become an established voice among the liberal media.

But during the period when she was busy building her media business, Arianna had suffered a personal crisis. In 2007, during the nonstop days of growing her start-up, Arianna had awakened on the floor of her home office in a pool of blood. She'd passed out, fallen, and broken her cheekbone. "In the wake of my collapse, I found myself going from doctor to doctor, from brain MRI to CAT scan to echocardiogram, to find out if there was any underlying medical condition beyond exhaustion," she later wrote. "There wasn't."[6]

The episode made Arianna acutely aware that, as she puts it, "I had bought into what I now consider the delusion that burnout is the price you must pay to achieve your goals. What I came to learn was that, as the science shows, we don't have to burn out to succeed."[7] Over the next few years, she began spreading this cautionary message to others, first in a commencement address at Smith College, then in her 2014 book, *Thrive*. In 2016, she stepped down from the *Huffington Post* (which she'd sold to AOL for $315 million) to launch Thrive Global, a website focused on "behavior change" that publishes content and consults with Fortune 500 companies. "We are at an inflection point, and something very important is happening in the culture," she told *Fortune* the month she launched. "And that's what made me take the very tough decision to leave, you know, a media company that I built from scratch."[8]

In personal branding, this may seem like a radical pivot. But because Arianna had a well-established brand as a powerful thinker (her *meta brand*), she had the flexibility to make this leap without having to rewrite her meta brand.

"When making a decision like the one to found *Thrive Global* . . . I've never thought about it in terms of my personal brand," she told me.[9] "I've just followed my passions. And one that's been a through-line to my entire life has been my love of helping people engage and connect. . . . So in that sense, *Thrive Global* was less of a shift than a natural progression—it's about going beyond raising awareness and helping people make real changes in their lives."

Arianna notes that her shift in focus was aided by the authenticity of her narrative—that her interest in wellness began with a legitimate crisis brought on by exhaustion. "My collapse made me stop, step back, and realize how far off course our modern culture had veered from what—according to both science and ancient wisdom—really makes us happy and fulfilled," she told me. It became an important data point in the evolution of how both her friends and the broader public came to understand Arianna and her work.

Personal brands matter throughout your professional life, but they become especially important during low moments. Politicians who are voted out of office may suddenly find they have many fewer friends calling; star athletes may feel an acute loss of stature when they retire. It's during these moments that one's personal brand—one built on consistent and authentic professional interactions—matters most.

RECAP

▶ Choose the five attributes you would like to have associated with your personal brand. Behave in ways that allow others to see these qualities in you.

▶ Eschew social media and self-promotion as foundational for building a powerful, durable, reliable personal brand.

▶ Don't let your brand limit you to the familiar. Understand your meta brand and its possibilities.

PROTECTING YOUR PERSONAL LIFE

No success in public life can compensate for failure in the home.

—J. E. McCulloch,
Home: The Savior of Civilization (1924)

Very early in my career, soon after I'd joined Trammell Crow Company, I got a call on a Sunday afternoon. To my surprise, the voice on the other end was Trammell Crow, the company's founder. Trammell asked me to come to the office that afternoon to go over some details on an important deal.

I had just seconds to respond to the question—which was actually phrased more as a directive, with no question mark at the end. I was torn. I'd been working long hours during my first weeks in the new job, and I hadn't been spending enough time with my wife, who was pregnant with our first child. All week I'd been promising her that this Sunday afternoon would belong to just the two of us.

Still, this was a request from the fellow whose name is on the door, and this phone conversation constituted one of our first professional interactions. Quickly, I mustered my courage. "Sir, I'm sorry, but I reserve Sundays for my family," I said. "I'm happy to come in as early as you like on Monday morning, but I am not available to work on Sundays."

Crow didn't sound pleased by my answer, but he accepted it. That was the last time he ever asked me to work on a Sunday. Despite that, over time he became a mentor, and I went on to become the firm's managing partner—in part, I'm convinced, because of the clear boundaries I set the first time I'd faced this request.

Entrepreneurial leaders must manage their time effectively—and that's true both in the office and at home. If you're good with your office day-planner (or Outlook, or whatever electronic calendaring device you prefer), get good with your personal one too. Time for family and friends, for health, for learning, for recreation, and for reflection all need scheduling. Work priorities may have to take a back seat when more important ones won't.

If you spend time around successful leaders, you will discover many of them have created imaginative hacks for building and protecting the boundaries around their personal time. Kent Thiry is the former CEO at DaVita—and one of the most intentional leaders I know. He keeps track of how many nights he's away from home on business and how many nights he misses dinner due to work commitments. Each quarter he analyzes the data, sets goals, and makes adjustments as necessary. John Doerr, the legendary venture capitalist (an early backer of Google and Amazon, among many others) does the same thing.

I think about these conflicting priorities through the metaphor of juggling. Everybody is juggling a bunch of things in their lives. Some are rubber balls; some are glass balls. If you drop a rubber ball, it bounces, so there's no harm. If you drop a glass ball, it will shatter and cannot be repaired. The trick to juggling is to always differentiate the rubber balls from the glass balls—and to never drop the glass ones.

At the same time, I occasionally meet business leaders who achieve high marks at work but whose personal lives seem sad and unfulfilling. I am not alone in this observation. Clayton Christensen, a Harvard Business School professor whom I've gotten to know while serving together on the board at Franklin Covey, wrote a book called *How Will You Measure Your Life?*

The book stemmed from Christensen's observations at his business school reunions, where he saw classmates who were building successful careers but were failing outside of work. At his tenth reunion, he recalls, "There were . . . numerous stories of divorce or unhappy marriages. I remember one classmate who hadn't talked to his children in years. . . . Another was on her third marriage since we'd graduated."[1] At his twenty-fifth and thirtieth business school reunions, he met more classmates whose dismal personal lives contrasted with their professional success. He witnessed the same thing at reunions of the Rhodes scholars with whom he'd attended Oxford. At least two former classmates wound up in prison.

The specifics of each of these unhappy cases is surely unique. (As Tolstoy put it, "Each unhappy family is unhappy in its own way."[2]) But Christensen sees a broader trend at work. People who wind up as Rhodes scholars or attending Harvard Business School tend to be focused, goal-oriented, type A people who know how to work hard. This disposition, which helps them excel in one part of life, can lead them to neglect other parts. "The danger for high achieving people is that they'll unconsciously allocate their resources to activities that yield the most immediate, tangible accomplishments," Christensen writes.[3] "Many of us are wired with a high need for achievement, and your career is going to be the most immediate way to pursue that. In our own internal resource allocation process, it will be incredibly tempting to invest every extra hour of time or ounce of energy in whatever activity yields the clearest and most immediate evidence that we're achieving something. Our careers provide such evidence in spades."[4]

Investing time in friends, family, church, or hobbies can feel somewhat less tangible. While a boss can give you a promotion or a raise, a strong friendship offers no external markers or milestones of accomplishment. Raising children is the ultimate long-term investment; very often, the day-to-day work of a parent can feel frustrating or unrewarding, especially during the sometimes sullen teenage years.

The way to deal with this risk of overinvesting in work and underinvesting in life outside the office is to create systems and boundaries that prevent a misallocation. That's what this map is about.

One important note about the way we think and talk about this issue: Many people refer to this entire topic as "balancing work and family," a phrase that contains built-in normative assumptions about how people *should* be spending nonwork hours. To be sure, my own life—a marriage of forty-seven years, seven children, twenty-six grandchildren—fits these assumptions. For me, family is the bull's-eye at the center of my life and priorities.

But I recognize this won't be true for every reader. Around the world, people are marrying later (if at all), and rates of childbearing are dropping. Particularly for young professionals in their twenties and early thirties, balancing work with a personal life is less likely to involve parental responsibilities or a spouse than it did when I was that age. In this chapter, I talk about family as my nonwork priority; however, I see this as a placeholder. I recognize that other readers may have completely different goals and aspirations for what they want to accomplish outside of work.

So whether your personal life centers on a close group of friends, a softball team, CrossFit, volunteer work, a book club, dating, poker night, or fantasy football, and no matter if marriage and children don't fit anywhere in your life plan, the imperative remains: cultivate and invest in relationships outside of work, and create systems and rituals that build guardrails around this precious part of life.

When it comes to time management, Stephen Covey recommended that people think of their lives like a big mason jar. After fitting in "the big rocks"—the important stuff—fill the remaining space with pebbles, then sand. And there's still a lot of room for water—the analogy's least important matters, filling the interstices.

For me, the big rocks were always my kids. As a parent, when you miss a concert, soccer game, or parent-teacher conference, you've lost an opportunity that won't come back. Worse yet, your absence during these moments sends a message to impressionable young people. Being with my kids meant sleeping a little less, missing occasional business trips, and leaving the briefcase in the car—all worth it in a big-rock scheme of life. My kids also learned that I was busy and had commitments to other important matters, helping them appreciate our time together.

Rituals and traditions can be a way to protect and routinize time together. In my family, a couple of rituals helped keep a group of busy people connected. Many Saturday mornings, I used to sit my younger children in my lap and interview them, starting with a simple question: "Tell me about you this past week." A minute or two might go by in silence. But I waited. Experience had taught me that I rarely had to prod. Most weekends, my children talked about an emotional event involving a friend or teacher. Someone had hurt their feelings. A teacher said something nice. They made a new friend. These weekly conversations continued as long as the child was small enough to sit in my lap.

Each New Year's Eve, we participated in a different family ritual: using a roll of butcher paper, we reviewed the preceding year while creating a calendar, marking personal memories or milestones month by month. One son received his Eagle Scout badge. A daughter won a spelling bee. We took another child to New York or a different child to see Omaha Beach at Normandy. (We have always made special efforts to take children on solo trips, to allow for one-on-one parent-child bonding time.) One year, a daughter transcribed forty years of these New Year's scrolls into a single document—one that's over thirty feet long and contains hundreds of special moments that would have been forgotten if not for our tradition of setting aside a holiday to reflect on (and record) what happened during the prior year.

Along with rituals and traditions, another tool can help increase the odds that busy professionals will invest sufficiently in their personal lives: a written plan, a set of goals, or a mission statement.

It may seem overwrought to apply these formal management tools to one's personal life. But to me, it makes perfect sense. I would never consider starting a business without a business plan, without a clear notion of what "winning" meant, or without measurement along the way. Why would I attempt what I consider life's greatest summit—building a successful family—absent the same mindful, intentional approach?

Instead of just winging it when it came to raising a family, being a spouse, and playing a role as father, many years ago I wrote a document I called a "Family Philosophy." Knowing what I know today, I could do a better job. But as a thirtysomething executive struggling with the pressures of family and work, I did the best I could, mindful of the wisdom of D-Day architect Dwight D. Eisenhower, who said: "Plans are worthless, but planning is everything."[5]

When writing this document, the key questions I asked myself were *What am I solving for? What would winning look like?* Once I decided to solve for the eventual maturity of my kids, I broke down the process into component parts—just as I might design a business project with deliverables, timetables, resource allocations, and ongoing reviews.

My wife and I decided that our success as parents would ultimately be measured by our children's maturity along six dimensions: spiritual development, intellectual development, physical development, emotional development, character development, and skill development.

Using this framework, we then worked to "operationalize" it by creating lists of family and individual activities that would help our children achieve these outcomes. Music lessons, participation in sports, learning foreign languages, volunteering, working minimum-wage jobs, and attending church all figured into this system. To be sure, many families encourage their children to do these things, but our approach was pretty systematic; we saw them as a means to an end.

The document we created, which has evolved over forty years, became granular at times. Thus it contains lists of books, movies, and travel destinations we wanted each child to experience. Later, we invited kids to add their own metrics. When I have shared this document with my MBA students at Stanford, more than a few have laughed that they were grateful not to have grown up in the Peterson family. But as applied in real life, this "philosophy" was much more flexible than one might suppose. Its most useful aspect was the framework for faster, more creative decision-making it afforded for us having "paid the price" to articulate it early on.

Indeed, there's nothing prescriptive about the specifics in our document; other individuals or families would surely construct something much different but equally valid. I simply imagined my own children joining the ranks of the most mature, well-adjusted, and perspicacious people I'd ever met, thought hard about the paths most likely to lead to that outcome, and tried to create a series of turn-by-turn directions to get them there. For my kids, *achieving maturity in all its dimensions* was the goal.

One important element of the process was that our kids had the sense that we were "about something." We weren't just picking them up from school, attending their games, and helping them with schoolwork while figuring out how to pay our mortgage and juggle other social and financial obligations. We had a plan, an objective, a mission—one that we'd taken the time to define as winning and that communicated a purpose beyond just getting through the day. We had a dream for each of them that was all about *them* becoming whatever they wanted to become, feeling self-confident and loved unconditionally.

For a young executive who risked feeling torn between work and home, the presence of goals and objectives at home helped activate my ambition and need for achievement—and helped prevent me from falling into the trap of sacrificing personal goals for more easily quantifiable professional goals. By drawing boundaries, defining winning, creating goals and an operational plan, my duties as father—ones I might otherwise have seen as a *competing* claim—turned into a sort of gyroscope whose angular momentum allowed me to maintain life's proper orientation, to keep me from getting lost in the claims and pressures that buffet so many leaders. Just as pilots are trained to compensate for the forces that cause planes to pitch, roll, and yaw, I found that having a clearly articulated family philosophy kept me from becoming disoriented in inclement weather.

Tension between home and office can be especially acute early in a career. All professionals go through periods when they are working more than they should. I learned that balance in life or on a beam will suffer the occasional wobble—or even a fall. Most of us will look back later with some regret about how we spent our time as the price of a busy life. So don't worry if you're out of balance for a season; just don't abandon the imperative of rebalancing.

My children are grown now; the youngest is twenty-eight. All are married and raising their own children.

This introduces an obvious question: How well did our intentional, goal-oriented system of operationalizing our parenting goals work out? If this family philosophy represented an investment, what's the return on it?

It's hard to give an answer without the risk of bragging. Nonetheless, I'm proud of my children. As a group, they have graduated from some of the world's finest colleges and graduate schools, embarked on careers that make a difference in the world, made smart choices when choosing spouses, and avoided the temptation to overinvest in their work at the expense of their nonwork lives.

To be sure, each has suffered setbacks and faces challenges. When they do, they have the resilience and character to come back from them. But more important than any of their visible achievements, Diana and I are proud of the people they have become.

One needn't have a spouse or children to feel a sense of pride and accomplishment in the life one builds outside of work. Deep friendships, civic leadership, volunteer work that makes an impact—there are many realms in which one can leave a mark outside of work. That's why it's so important to set limits on how much of your life you will devote to your career.

David Brooks, the *New York Times* columnist, found that although he'd attained a certain amount of career success, he felt he wanted to be a better human—and he set about doing the work to achieve that goal. Ultimately, he used those experiences to write a book called *The Road to Character*. He described some of its conclusions in a column in the *Times* three days before the book released. "There [are] two sets of virtues, the résumé virtues and the eulogy virtues," he wrote. "The résumé virtues are the skills you bring to the marketplace. The eulogy virtues are the ones that are talked about at your funeral—whether you were kind, brave, honest or faithful. Were you capable of deep love? We all know that the eulogy virtues are more important than the résumé ones. But our culture and our educational systems spend more time teaching the skills and strategies you need for career success. . . . Many of us are clearer on how to build an external career than on how to build inner character."[6]

As a parent, I am proud of my children's résumés—but I'm prouder of their character. Likewise, I am proud of my own career achievements—but if anyone were ever tempted to eulogize me, I'd hope they would reference what I accomplished when I wasn't at work—when I was cultivating friendships, serving others, and building a family. I am able to maintain this hope largely because I intentionally set out to invest deeply in my family and personal life.

Every entrepreneurial leader needs a plan to help him or her escape the strong gravitational pull of work. The tools I've described, as idiosyncratic as they are, can help. Focusing on building your eulogy virtues can too.

RECAP

▶ Set boundaries on your work to make room for nonwork interests and commitments.

▶ Operationalize those commitments, giving them the same priority you give to professional assignments and career rewards.

▶ Expect to be "out-of-balance" during certain seasons, but don't abandon the need to reprioritize and rebalance your priorities.

CREATE
A MISSION

Mission gives meaning, clarity, and priority to collective actions. Mission answers the question "What would winning look like?" Mission clarity puts everyone on the same page and resolves conflicts. Having the right mission is key to assembling the right team. A compelling mission identifies what the market needs and what stakeholders can bring to your efforts. A team without mission is one without focus, priorities, and deadlines—and one condemned to failure. A team aligned on the same trek is belayed and committed to helping each other—and is already halfway to the summit.

FINDING MEANING

A business that makes nothing but money is a poor business.
—Henry Ford, as quoted in the Mansfield (Ohio)
News Journal (August 3, 1965)

Most people aren't working for just a paycheck. In an economy in which highly skilled team members have so many options, they are effectively volunteering to work for one company or another. As they consider their choices, they ask themselves: Does this work matter? Is it consistent with my values? Does it have meaning?

Research shows that when team members believe in the mission of the organization, they perform better. Working alongside people who find meaning in their work is also more fun for everyone. Mission statements alone won't spark this emotional connection, but done well, they can be a useful tool.

For evidence of this, recall a story from the 1960s. With great fanfare, President Kennedy had announced before Congress a new mission for the Space Race: To "land a man on the moon and return him safely to earth" by the end of the decade. Not long after making that announcement, Kennedy made his first visit to NASA headquarters. During the tour, according to an unverified, but oft-repeated story, Kennedy encountered a janitor working quietly in a hallway and stopped to introduce himself. "Hi, I'm Jack

Kennedy," the president said. "What are you doing?" The janitor replied, "Well, Mr. President, I'm helping put a man on the moon."[1] Because this worker had internalized the transcendent mission of his organization, he found even the quotidian task of cleaning the floors meaningful—a part of the Herculean task of getting men into space. Wouldn't you want the lowest-level employee in your organization feeling that same sense of pride and focus?

Part of the job of an entrepreneurial leader is to formulate and articulate this mission so that everyone understands it, remembers it, and owns it. When this happens, people sense their work has meaning.

Good mission statements are simple, powerful, and emotive. Here are some examples:

1. **Disney:** "To entertain, inform and inspire people around the globe through the power of unparalleled storytelling."
2. **Amazon:** "To be the Earth's most customer-centric company."
3. **Nordstrom:** "To prove our customers with the best possible service."
4. **Costco:** "To continually provide our members with quality goods and services at the lowest possible prices."
5. **Google:** "Organize the world's information and make it universally accessible and useful."
6. **Nike:** "To bring inspiration and innovation to every athlete in the world."
7. **eBay:** "To be the world's favorite destination for discovering great value and unique selection."
8. **Uniqlo:** "To create truly great clothing with new and unique value and to enable people all over the world to experience the joy, happiness and satisfaction of wearing such great clothes."
9. **McDonald's:** "To serve safe and delicious food to our customers each and every day."
10. **Starbucks:** "To inspire and nurture the human spirit—one person, one cup, and one neighborhood at a time."

Cynics—those who celebrate the negative view of business portrayed in the *Dilbert* comic strips or the television show *The Office*—may discount mission statements as a collection of meaningless words whose aim is corporate propaganda. In some cases, this may be true. But in most cases, it's not. When an entrepreneurial leader chooses the right words to express the mission, communicates them effectively, models the right behaviors, and takes steps to align the workforce and culture around this mission, the results can be dramatic.

When not done well, however, mission or vision statements can be demotivating. Imagine you work in one of the following four organizations. You're given one of the mission statements that follow. Study it for thirty seconds, then try to recite it back. Now imagine using it while recruiting new team members, establishing core values, and setting up great execution. Try to explain how each set of words might differentiate it from any number of competitors:

1. "Provide our customers with the most convenient access to media entertainment, including movie and game entertainment delivered through multiple distribution channels such as our stores, by mail, vending and kiosks, online and at home. We believe [we] offer customers a value-priced entertainment experience, combining the broad product depth of a specialty retailer with local neighborhood convenience."

2. "To make sure that we are all working in the same direction, each of us must live and breathe [our company's] values and use them as a guidepost for our actions and decisions."

3. "Improve the lives of our members and customers by providing quality services, products and solutions that earn their trust and build lifetime relationships."

4. "Make every associate and customer feel Welcome, Important and Appreciated, which paves the way for a positive work atmosphere at our corporate headquarters and an inviting shopping experience in our stores."

All are vague. Many are too long. Some are merely descriptive of the status quo, lost in the weeds of the current product offering. Some, in contrast, leave you with no clue what the company offers customers. Few are distinctive, poetic, or memorable.

The company behind each, in order: Blockbuster, Circuit City, Sears, and A&P.

All of these firms have filed for bankruptcy. It would be unfair to trace their failure to a mushy and indistinctive mission or vision statement. Still, when the labored-over phrase that is meant to be the company's rallying cry is interchangeable with those of any other enterprise, it's not a good sign.

I'm fortunate to have seen firsthand the power of a great mission at JetBlue. Prior to starting the company, David Neeleman had helped lead another airline that he sold to Southwest. After that deal closed, he'd gone to work for Southwest and its legendary founder, Herb Kelleher. During his five-month stay there, Neeleman studied the company's economic model, which allowed it to offer flights to passengers at low cost.

During this era, in the mid-1990s, airplanes had begun to feel like crowded, expensive buses in the sky. Whatever glamour surrounded air travel in the 1950s and 1960s had faded in the two decades since deregulation. Neeleman's goal was to take the Southwest low-fare model and transform it into an enjoyable and inclusive experience, with more focus on passenger comfort and caring service. Some of the specific ways to do that were already on our drawing boards. With wider seats covered in comfortable leather, live television offered free to every passenger, and free snacks, Neeleman had created clear ways to operationalize the JetBlue offering into a distinctive value proposition. The mission he'd chosen—"To bring humanity back to air travel"—perfectly captured his aims. Getting this mission right is one of the reasons JetBlue got off to such a strong launch.

Getting these words right is harder than it looks. Eight years after JetBlue's founding, its board (of which I was a brand-new chair) decided to update the mission statement. During an off-site meeting, directors spent an hour trying to craft a pithy, meaningful phrase that captured the aim of what was then a $2 billion airline. Our results sounded like our auditors had drafted it. The key line declared that our airline would become "the premier value-based carrier in the Americas." We used the phrase internally for a time but quickly recognized it was not simple or powerful or emotive—and that not a single customer, crewmember, or shareholder would find meaning in that phrase. So we tried to think harder about what constituted "winning."

After Neeleman left the company, his successor, David Barger, wanted to expand the mission, and it became even simpler. The new mission became: "Serving humanity." This made sense not only for simplicity, but because JetBlue's business was expanding. As we began offering vacation packages, for instance, we weren't just in the airline business anymore. Now under our third CEO, Robin Hayes, JetBlue is beginning the process of offering transatlantic travel and broader services, so we've again begun rewriting the mission statement.

Whenever I encounter a first-rate business, I'm struck by how frequently there's a simple and compelling mission at the root of what the company is trying to achieve. When Bill Gates founded Microsoft, this high-level mission setting included teams committed to "a computer on every desk and in every home"[2]—a mission which Microsoft has gone on to achieve. When I talked with Stanford students who were joining the social networking startup Facebook in 2006 and 2007, their service had just a few million users (mostly college students) and was dwarfed by MySpace. Nonetheless, Facebook founder Mark Zuckerberg frequently talked about the company's mission ("To give people the power to share and make the world more open and connected"[3]) along with an audacious goal that some said bordered on the ridiculous: to have more than one billion people using the site, or about one in every seven humans on the planet. As ridiculous as that number sounded at the time, Zuckerberg over delivered—as I write this, Facebook's monthly user count stands at 2.38 billion.

Many leaders struggle with the difference between mission, vision, values, purpose, principles, goals, objectives, motto, philosophy, and tagline. They all sound like high-level expressions of what a team or organization stands for—a bit too high-minded for some, a bit irrelevant to the real work of the enterprise for others.

When I advise entrepreneurial leaders on how to approach the task of addressing the need for meaning in a pithy, memorable phrase, I suggest they focus on three related but similar notions: *mission*, *values*, and *tagline*.

Mission is the overarching objective the organization is trying to achieve. When I think about mission, I sometimes think of the phrase the officiant utters near the beginning of a traditional wedding service: "Dearly beloved, we are gathered here today . . ." The company's mission answers this implied question: What have we gathered here to accomplish?

Values, on the other hand, are where you spend your money, your time, and your mind share. Consider Apple. While its mission statement (which I won't take the space to quote here) is too long, too focused on individual products, and not very inspiring, its values, as articulated by current CEO Tim Cook, are a strong example of how a firm can express its core values in a compelling way:

1. We are constantly focusing on *innovating*.
2. We believe in the *simple* not the complex.
3. We believe that we need to *own and control* the primary technologies behind the products that we make, and participate only in markets where we can make a significant contribution.
4. We believe in saying no to thousands of projects, so that we can really *focus on the few* that are truly *important* and *meaningful* to us.
5. We believe in deep *collaboration* and *cross-pollination* of our groups, which allow us to innovate in a way that others cannot.
6. And frankly, we don't settle for anything less than *excellence* in every group in the company, and we have the *self-honesty* to admit when we're wrong and the *courage* to change.

One helpful way to think about developing your team's mission, values, and tagline is to try to find phrases that succinctly and uniquely describe three things:

1. *What* we do.
2. *How* we do it.
3. *Who* we are.

An entrepreneurial leader who can create a single, memorable phrase that highlights the essence of his or her organization and what makes it different from all others has found pixie dust—something employees will recite, investors will back, and customers will turn into a habit.

When an organization has an effective mission, odds are most employees could recite a reasonably close version of it. Mission statements give focus—usually around a word or two, a unique deliverable at the heart of the mission. Not all are short; but they all connect to what people experience with the brand and represent a uniqueness that most people inside and outside the enterprise would recognize as setting it apart from its competitors.

In an era when so many business leaders think and speak about the necessity of "doing well by doing good," it's worth taking a moment to address the advisability of adding social responsibility to a mission. Those who claim virtue as a part of their mission—to say explicitly they are making the world a better place—risk confusion. It's fine to list virtues in a separate statement, but the mission—the objective, the highest purpose of the enterprise—is not a forum in which to demonstrate integrity to the world. Claiming virtue as a mission risks cynicism.

Mission statements should be short, unambiguous, and meaningful. Good ones leave no one guessing about what business the company is in. (For instance, the mission statement of General Motors surely would be better if it included something to do with *vehicles*.) When contrasting the mission statements of successful with unsuccessful companies, I think of Oliver Wendell Holmes Jr.'s words: "The only simplicity for which I would give a straw is that which is on the other side of the complex—not that which never has divined it."⁴ Those who have not wrestled complexity to the ground to expose the essence of their firm, their institution, or their family have fallen short. The best ones show a one-of-a-kind mission or a striving to be the best at what others are also striving to do.

Finally, taglines are different but derivative. The tagline is meant for external consumption. It's how your customer reads your mission. It's a catchphrase or slogan that's used in the company's advertising and branding.

Aimed at an external audience, taglines are often produced in consultation with an ad agency. Very often, they aren't in place until well after a company launches its original product—and very often, they change every few years.

Taglines share an important similarity with mission and values: when a company finds the right one, it can be an important element in helping it discover, hone, and communicate its essence and describe its uniqueness. As with missions, taglines are most effective if they're short and memorable. Done well, taglines can be another tool to help employees and customers find meaning in what the company is trying to accomplish.

Here are some of my favorite taglines:

1. **Jimmy John's:** "Freaky Fast Freaky Fresh."
2. **Whole Foods:** "Whole Foods—Whole People—Whole Planet."
3. **Allstate:** "You're in good hands with Allstate."
4. **Spotify:** "Music for everyone."
5. **L.L.Bean:** "The outside is inside everything we make."
6. **Nike:** "Just do it."
7. **United States Marine Corps:** "The Few. The Proud."

One needn't have a formal mission statement to have a mission. My father found meaning in his work as a research scientist. He studied agriculture and biology, working to breed new strains of onions, carrots, and cucumbers. Many of the projects he pursued aimed to create vegetables with higher levels of vitamins—for example, a new kind of carrot with more beta-carotene to help malnourished children in developing countries overcome the scourge of nutritional blindness.

To my father, this work was meaningful. It became his personal mission, his own version of trying to put a man on the moon. He believed he had the best job in the world, and if given a chance to trade places and careers with Warren Buffett, he would have said no.

That's the power of finding meaning in one's work and making it your personal mission.

RECAP

▶ Work hard to articulate a clear purpose, a desired end result, what winning looks like.

▶ Differentiate between (1) your values—where you spend your time, money, and mind share, (2) your mission—what describes your unique purpose, and (3) your tagline—what your customers will see as your "promise" to them.

▶ Extend this notion of mission to everything you do.

STEP 2

SETTING
MAD GOALS

A man who chases two rabbits catches neither.
—Proverb

A mission statement that captures the essence of an enterprise is made real and motivating by its goals.

When I was in college, I learned the story of John Goddard, the American explorer who became famous for something that happened when he was just fifteen years old. Sitting at his kitchen table in Los Angeles in 1940, Goddard wrote three words on a piece of paper: My Life List.[1] Underneath it, he carefully wrote out 127 experiences he hoped to achieve during his lifetime.

On the surface, the goals he listed—which included running a sub–five-minute mile, climbing the world's tallest mountains, and reading the entire *Encyclopedia Britannica*—seemed a tad ambitious, especially for a teenager. But between that moment and his death in 2013, Goddard set out to systematically check off the goals he'd set. He kayaked the entire length of the Nile and Congo Rivers. He survived a plane crash, quicksand, and an attack by Egyptian pirates. He set records as a jet pilot.[2] Upon his death, the *Los Angeles Times* compared him to Indiana Jones, writing: "Each goal was meticulously ticked off as he reached it, from 'watch a cremation ceremony in Bali' (No. 91) to 'milk a poisonous snake' (No. 117)."[3] Goddard didn't achieve everything on his list—he never made it to the top of Mount Everest or landed on the moon, among the eighteen objectives he missed. But by purposely setting goals and working to meet them, he lived a life marked by extraordinary experiences and achievement.

Few of us live our lives in this manner. Too many of us make wishes—vague, adolescent hopes without sufficient power to change the trajectory of a life, a team, or a business. Goals, on the other hand, can be measured, are associated with deadlines, and come with an allocation of resources, an assessment of trade-offs, and a sense of accountability. Unlike wishes, goals produce meaningful results.

Knowing how to establish great goals is a key skill for any entrepreneurial leader who hopes to build something durable.

Having launched or backed some 250 companies, helped develop over twenty-three hundred real estate projects, and served on dozens of boards, I can say with confidence that the successful ones were based on clear goals and the metrics that surround them. Likewise, my biggest failures were mired in objectives as vague at the outset as they were predictive of failure in the end.

When I make goals, I imagine—in as much detail as possible—a winning outcome. The key is to imagine—with specificity—how the world will look upon achievement of the goal. How will I feel? Who will be my allies? My detractors? What will be the rewards/costs to all? How would I describe success in a sentence? And how would I quantify the outcome?

The best goals share three qualities: They are *memorable*, *aligned*, and *doable*. I refer to these as MAD goals.

The Power of Memorable (M): As an in-class exercise, I ask students in a course I teach at Stanford to present their personal goals to the class as a leader might to a team. One year, two students expressed goals in terms of health and personal fitness. One went over an impressive set of metrics around making sure to eat right, exercise regularly, and get plenty of sleep. The other presented a goal in a single phrase: "Running a marathon at age thirty-five faster than I'd run it at age twenty-five." At the end of the quarter, I asked students to recall classmates' goals. Everyone recalled the marathoner's. Years later, I meet students who still do. (Almost no one recalled the student with multiple health metrics.) And when I asked the marathoner about it a decade later, that goal had been achieved.

The best way to make goals memorable is to keep them short, imbue them with compelling emotional content, and make them measurable.

The Necessity of Alignment (A): Alignment is the set of forces that get a team moving in the same direction. Goals are aligned when they are in keeping with core values. Without alignment—that is, without connection from hearts to minds and reinforcement from thought to action all the way from the values that move people to the measurements that tell them they're on track—the odds of achieving any goal diminish quickly. And goals set but not achieved are dispiriting. Thus carefully choosing the right goals is essential to having a credible, inspiring, and effective mission. (You'll learn more about alignment in the next section of this book.)

The Imperative of Doability (D): When I became chairman at JetBlue in 2008, the airline was losing $84 million per year. My first act was to organize an off-site strategy meeting, at which I asked various board members to help us develop our objectives. Frank Sica, former head of Soros Private Equity Partners, proposed the goal of earning $1 per share. I wondered how that was doable. But by assigning champions, budgets, time frames, and deliverables to each—the four-part screen for assessing doability—I could see a path forward, and we eventually met and exceeded that mark.

Different people have different systems for setting goals, but when you scratch beneath the surface, they tend to share similarities. John Doerr, the legendary venture capitalist who was an initial investor in Amazon, Google, and Twitter, calls his system OKRs—for Objectives and Key Results. In his book *Measure What Matters*, he recalls learning the system from Andy Grove at Intel. Years later, Doerr taught it to the Google founders in the early days, when all the company's employees—about thirty people—could fit around a Ping Pong table. "An OBJECTIVE, I explained, is simply WHAT is to be achieved, no more and no less," Doerr writes. "By definition, objectives are significant, concrete, action-oriented, and (ideally) inspirational. . . . KEY RESULTS benchmark and monitor HOW we get to the objective. Effective KRs are specific and time-bound, aggressive yet realistic. Most of all, they are measurable and verifiable." Doerr quotes former Yahoo CEO Marissa Mayer: "It's not a key result unless it has a number."[4]

Many people mistake tasks for goals. Goals are what you are trying to achieve; tasks are what go on a daily to-do list to work toward goals. Many young leaders sit atop an infinite to-do list, thinking they have goals. Look at the list one first-time CEO generated when I asked her to lay out her goals for the coming year:

1. Fill out the fall product line
2. Update the website
3. Expand the line of credit
4. Complete employee reviews
5. Reorganize the sales force
6. Cut back Region A
7. Expand Region B
8. Develop employee training

Her actual list included another fifteen similar items. They were, of course, not goals (endpoints); they were (in-process) tasks. If properly organized, they *might* be supportive of a goal.

When it comes to goal setting, entrepreneurial leaders borrow heavily from the tool kit of managers and executives: they are ruthless about setting objectives, keeping their team focused on a clear, compelling, and *limited* set of big goals—ideally, three each. The entrepreneurial leader is the guardian and evangelist for the organization and its priorities. It's up to her to keep the goals in neon letters so everyone from the C-suite to the street level can see them.

By contrast, I used to work with a very successful lawyer. He was a wonderful fellow—brilliant, likeable, hardworking. However, he spent all day working his in-box. Whatever came into his in-box was the work he would do, without thought to the larger goals he hoped to achieve. His work felt urgent, but it wasn't always truly important. Because he wasn't attending to important work, crises blew up from time to time—and even when they didn't, he often accomplished little of a durable nature.

I started out my career the same way. I'd just spent two years studying for an MBA, working on whatever case professors assigned me. However, I soon learned that in most real-world managerial jobs, a supervisor doesn't tell you exactly what to do every day. I came to realize that figuring out what to do, in what order, and how to do it was the essence of what I had to do as an entrepreneurial leader.

Without great goals, people see only hurdles in front of tasks. Thus they often put obstacles—not priorities—at the top of their worry lists.

Goal setting need not be complicated. But it *must* end in clarity. When Winston Churchill was installed as prime minister of Great Britain on May 13, 1940, he delivered a short speech to the House of Commons in which he said: "You ask, what is our aim? I can answer in one word: It is victory, victory at all costs, victory in spite of all terror, victory, however long and hard the road may be; for without victory, there is no survival."[5]

Churchill repeated his goal five times in thirty-nine words. His two-fingered salute became the "V for victory" sign. His symbol was the bulldog. He became the walking embodiment of an indomitable determination to achieve victory. When Armenian Canadian photographer Yousuf Karsh sought to capture this human embodiment of a goal, he snatched Churchill's cigar from his grasp and snapped the shot at the instant of his glowering. No other photograph captures so well his "victory at all costs" persona. It has since become one of the most iconic images of WWII—a photo that hangs in my office to remind me of goal clarity and indomitability.[6]

Jim Collins and Jerry Porras call objectives that drive winning BHAGs—short for "Big, Hairy, Audacious Goals."[7] Gary Hamel and C. K. Prahalad call them, more prosaically, "strategic intent."[8] Whatever they're called, good leaders craft objectives to encourage people to stretch beyond "what is" to "what could be." Because they often see beyond the company's existing resources and capabilities, they set goals that create a sense of discovery, a sense of direction, even the intimation of destiny. They inspire us to reach farther than anyone thought possible.

After more than four decades of research around the power of clarity in producing hoped-for results, the evidence is unequivocal. When leaders create and implement well-designed goals, people not only focus on the right priorities and increase their own efforts, they also tend to be more persistent and confident, and happier with their jobs. Great goals relieve boredom, help people develop better strategies, increase their enjoyment of work and, in many cases, boost job satisfaction.[9]

As an entrepreneurial leader, you might expect resistance to creating great goals. Many resistors approach goal setting in a half-hearted, perfunctory fashion. Others simply avoid it altogether. After all, once someone makes a goal public, there's always the risk of not reaching it.

People resist setting goals for five common reasons: (1) they fear failure; (2) they're nervous about having to make sacrifices; (3) they worry about the missed opportunities of pursuing one goal instead of another; (4) they obsess over costs; or (5) they prefer to pursue vague, unmeasured outcomes.

The cost of lousy, uninspiring goals is indeed high. Resources are wasted as time and attention are spent on superfluous activities. High priorities are held hostage to low priorities. Customers lose confidence, investors pull out, and the best employees move elsewhere. Most pernicious is the political infighting as people scramble for resources and resort to political gamesmanship in the absence of clarity around objectives.

Leaders who overcome this resistance and set out to create MAD goals must overcome these common problems:

1. **Having too many goals.** Goal abundance can overwhelm and frustrate people.

2. **Not having time frames.** Research on goal setting indicates that activities expand to fill the time available. Effective goals are time bound.

3. **Failing to communicate goals.** By not sharing goals, leaders not only miss out on advice or moral support but also communicate a lack of seriousness about goal setting.

4. **Overlooking interim goals.** When managing goals with a long horizon (two to five years, for example), make them psychologically meaningful by establishing interim wins.

5. **Failing to cluster goals.** It's important to group goals in meaningful ways, cascading smoothly from one achievement to the next.

6. **Failing to establish a line of sight.** When people lack a clear line of sight from their own responsibilities to the organization's high-level goals, they feel little connection to the organization and, consequently, to its victories or its problems.

7. **Being unwilling to adjust goals as circumstances change.** It makes little sense to stick with a goal if the situation changes dramatically. Yet this is what some presiders do, thinking that adjusting the goal will somehow suggest they made a mistake. Just as the difference between a budget (which stays fixed for a year) and a forecast (which is adjusted throughout the year) is the difference between goal setting and goal updating.

In contrast, great goal setters tend to use the following behaviors:

1. **They set goals that reflect actions that drive the business.** They choose goals that have a causal effect on multiple desired outcomes. For example, by setting a goal to reach a specific net promoter score (NPS) metric (which is a widely used measure of customer satisfaction), one can drive profit margins, customer loyalty, culture, and any number of other things that will build a moat around the brand. Goals measured by

ratios (revenue per employee, return on capital, and so forth) are a way to keep track of two measures at once by comparing their relationship as a numerator and a denominator. Look for goals like this—levers that can help achieve multiple positive outcomes.

2. **They distinguish goals from metrics.** The best way to avoid mixing goals with metrics is to ask why. For example, a common goal of businesses is to generate a market value of $X. Why? To reward shareholders. Why? To lower the cost of capital, increase the availability of capital, and create value for management options. Why? So the enterprise can attract talent, provide great service, and/or develop new products. Why? To delight customers. Why? To create an evergreen enterprise that achieves whatever are the objectives of most of the people in the company and/or those it serves so we can grow and be sustainably profitable. In the end, asking why over and over—as the writer Simon Sinek has suggested—may feel circular; however, it generally results in getting at the essence of what the team's most important goals really are.

3. **They limit the number of goals.** The main reason for limiting the number of goals is that everyone must be able to remember and recite them—everyone! Furthermore, having a limit forces prioritization and grouping. Don't stop until you've gotten your goals down to a number everyone can remember. Brainstorm. Group the potential goals by category. Figure out what are subordinate goals— ones that lead to the achievement of the broadest goal. And, finally, force rank the groupings from most to least critical—and cut off the list at number four.

4. **They make goals inspiring.** Wordsmith goals so they're inspiring as well as memorable. Create a visual image to make each goal memorable and inspiring. Who wouldn't remember

and be inspired by the goal of "Running a marathon faster at age thirty-five than I did at age twenty-five"?

5. If you work hard to make your goals memorable, aligned, and doable, the odds that your team will stretch to achieve them will go up dramatically.

RECAP

▶ Break down your mission into a limited number of goals that can be measured by meaningful, quantified, and time-bound deliverables.

▶ Ensure your goals align with your values and with the actions necessary to achieve them.

▶ Make sure everyone in your organization can recite its top three goals.

STEP 3

BUILDING ALIGNMENT

Convinced that behavior and conduct are every bit as
important as skills and expertise, I sought to build the firm
into an enduring, values-based institution.[1]
—Marvin Bower, *The Will to Manage* (1966)

During my first job out of business school, I worked for a brilliant PhD who'd previously been a consultant at McKinsey & Company. Despite his intellect and experience, he wasn't much of an entrepreneurial leader. His style was unpredictable, chaotic, and political. Connections to those in power seemed to trump the merit of ideas or even one's ability to consistently execute. Employees were under stress, partly because it was hard to predict what he might decide from one day to the next and partly because everything seemed a case of first impression. He seemed to be making it up as he went along, either having no discernable map or not sharing his priorities with the rest of us in a way we could help him achieve them.

Although he was hardly a role model for entrepreneurial leadership, I do remember him fondly for one reason. One day we were talking about the challenge of getting a diverse team all working toward the same goal. He referred me to a book that talked about this problem—one he insisted was the best business book he'd ever read. It was called *The Will to Manage* by Marvin Bower, who'd been managing partner at McKinsey from 1950 to 1967.

I recognized the name: one of my professors at Harvard Business School had referred to Bower as the father of modern management consulting. Bower, who died at age ninety-nine in 2003, had attended HBS and then joined the law firm Jones Day, where he worked with bondholders of companies facing bankruptcy. He became fascinated by why some companies succeeded and others failed. Three years later, Bower joined McKinsey, then a seven-year-old firm founded by James O. McKinsey, a former University of Chicago accounting professor. When McKinsey died just four years later, Bower, who was now in charge, moved the firm to New York and set it on a path of rapid and sustained growth.[2]

Although Bower's book, published in 1966,[3] was out of print, I tracked down a copy and read it. During this first reading, the book struck me as straightforward and logical—very McKinsey-like. "The key to corporate success is a leader with a strong will to manage, who inspires and requires people to work purposefully and effectively through simple and traditional managing processes that are integrated into a management program or system tailored to the nature and environment of the business," Bower writes.[4] He goes on to define management as "the activity or task of determining the objectives of an organization and then guiding the people and other resources of the organization in the successful achievement of those objectives."[5]

It all made sense, but on first reading, I found it prosaic and forgettable.

But every so often over the years, I picked it up and reread it—and eventually, I recognized the power of the simple system Bower is describing. Over time, I have come to see Bower's work as an essential and profound tutorial on an important element of what it takes to be an effective entrepreneurial leader.

In essence, Bower's system aligns a company's "never-changing philosophy"—its starting point for what it promises to deliver—with its core activities. For Bower, the first priority should reveal a "timeless objective," one that will devolve into a strategy—the (rarely changing) plans to achieve that primary objective.

For PepsiCo, this primary objective was, for many years, to "beat Coke." As noted previously, when David Neeleman started JetBlue, he was moved to bring humanity back to air travel by delivering value to customers and treating them like valued guests. This objective drove the strategy that defined our equipment, network, innovations, reservation system, and culture. These, in turn, defined how JetBlue delivered what we came to call "the JetBlue experience." And, of course, it drove us to measure not just financial results but customer delight and loyalty.

From "timeless objectives," whatever they are determined to be, Bower moves into the nuts-and-bolts of running stuff (setting policies, procedures, and standards; developing an organizational structure; hiring/coaching/firing; providing facilities; securing capital; developing communications; and so on). These are tactics—the who, how, where, and when decisions necessary to secure a strategy that will yield a desired outcome. It is at the tactical level that the wheels fall off, that conflicts emerge, and that confusion reigns in many businesses.

The driving element in Bower's hierarchy of concepts is what he terms "activating people." He defines this central element of business leadership this way: "Commanding and motivating people up and down the line to act in accordance with philosophy, policies, procedures, and standards in carrying out the plans of the company."[6] In other words, everything is the logical and predictable outgrowth of related activities. If you get everything aligned, things will tend to manage themselves. It was his notion of alignment that made me realize that most of the challenges I'd faced resulted from a disconnect between stated objectives and day-to-day practice.

Wherever values conflict with objectives, or when strategy doesn't support the objective, or the granular actions of individuals are at odds with an overarching strategy, or, finally, employees are rewarded for things that have nothing to do with the objective, people get confused. They figure that power determines priorities and conclude that politics are the operative system. In such organizations, the *who* is more important than the *what* when it comes to the *how*. Managing in this system is more for the politician and presider than for the entrepreneurial leader, who is constantly solving for innovation and on-time and on-budget results.

When I teach classes on entrepreneurial leadership, I always ask my students: What are you solving for? What is your objective? For those whose priority is to feel better, to vent, to demonstrate how smart they are or that their argument was more persuasive, they soon find they're pursuing something that's not the primary goal.

Those who have clarity around winning tend to listen. They tend to compromise, to allow other parties to win, to sort out conflicts, and to arrive at solutions that allow everyone to move on. This means that entrepreneurial leaders are rarely perfectionists. Instead, they are practical problem solvers who keep their eyes on primary objectives. The most successful among them pursue strategies that are relentlessly aimed at achieving measurable results consistent with core values.

This type of focus tends to build a great esprit de corps, one that ensures employees are respected members of a winning team that aspires to achieve something meaningful. These are simple skills anyone can learn. Using them with rigor, however, takes practice, insight, judgment, and the determination to eliminate distractions.

I put this entire feature of mission building under the rubric of achieving *alignment*. Put simply, alignment is the set of forces that get people moving in concert toward an agreed-upon goal, without much direct supervision or micromanagement by superiors. Setting goals that are consistent with values shared by people in the organization and reflective of their natural priorities would seem a simple and logical first step for any leader. For most, however, getting this right and building a system around it that is aligned with delivering on a common goal is hard. For the entrepreneurial leader it is the *sine qua non* of running stuff successfully. Just as $E = mc^2$ elegantly describes nature's correlation of energy to matter, the alignment of values, objectives, strategy, tactics, and controls captures the energy of the enterprise.

If a leader doesn't get his team aligned around the mission and the goals, everything falls apart. People begin putting self-interest ahead of team interests and winning games ahead of winning championships.

For that reason, building alignment is a quintessential task facing entrepreneurial leaders.

Over the years, based on my own experiences with leadership, I have simplified and renamed some of Bower's concepts, and arranged them in a hierarchy intended to remind the practitioner that while one must settle on a few core values that never change, there are lots of ways of measuring tactics—and they can change quarterly and by project. The following diagram represents the hierarchy of concepts to illustrate the power of alignment and how the various categories relate to each other. My students at Stanford have learned to call this the VOSTC map. (They pronounce it "Vo-Stick.") See below for my visual depiction of Bower's framework.

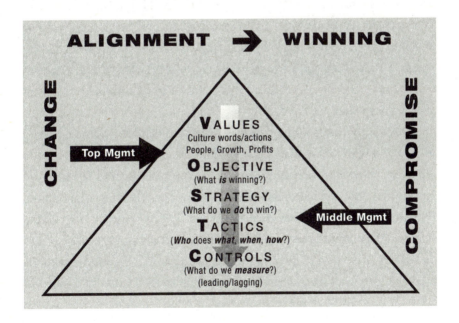

Under the headings—Values, Objective, Strategy, Tactics, Controls—I list core questions for the entrepreneurial leader and suggest that their answers should flow from values that include respect for people, a commitment to profitability, and a desire for controlled growth. For me, these are values for all seasons and for every organization, whether it's a commercial enterprise, a charity, or a family.

One of the principles my students find especially useful and compelling is to use this chart when they experience conflict. Conflicts that revolve around issues nearer the bottom of the pyramid—such as controls and tactics—are easier to solve through change and/or compromise. Conflicts that revolve around issues near the top (where they change less frequently)—especially values—may prove intractable.

Most conflicts are over tactics—who is going to do what, by when, and how? Often by bumping the discussion up a level—in this case to strategy—one will find that people are aligned and can develop insight into the tactical priorities that have them stymied.

If one finds disagreement over strategy, it's worth bumping the discussion up to objectives where, again, they will often find agreement. With a higher-level agreement, one may develop lower-level compromises. So long as one is not violating deeply held values, progress should be possible. If the conflict is over core values, over priorities, experience has taught me to end the relationship and move on to an enterprise or a team with shared values.

Consider politics, where many seem to have trouble finding compromise. Because of this, both sides attempt to convince us our disagreements are over core values. Speaking with people on both sides of the political spectrum, I've found that many not only share values and priorities around freedom, security, and prosperity but that they can agree on many of the strategies that secure them. While many disagree over the best tactics to achieve agreed-upon strategies, most find they can compromise, experiment, and keep talking with those with whom they initially disagreed. Most of our political debates in America are over strategy and tactics. There is broad agreement on the objectives and values of our nation. Sometimes by reestablishing objectives and prioritizing them, people fall into line behind strategies and tactics.

If one finds that a company, a nation, or a family no longer has the same objectives, it's worth reviewing values to see if one can agree on what matters most as a starting point for resetting objectives that can lead to a strategy, a series of tactics, and the metrics by which one can measure progress.

Without value alignment, however, it's over. Values conflicts are generally irreconcilable. When someone defects from his or her country of birth, or when someone who has devoted decades to a specific religion leaves that church, it is rarely over small-bore issues; it is usually due to a conflict over fundamental values. Values may not be immutable, but they are deeply ingrained—and as a result, people will rarely change or compromise them.

Over time, I've found that the best entrepreneurial leaders (1) hire for values; (2) set clear objectives that everyone understands; (3) come up with a strategy to achieve them that takes into account marketplace realities, organizational strengths, and the passions of the team; and then (4) develop the tactics to carry out the strategy.

It is at this tactical step highly skilled entrepreneurial leaders shine. They break tactics into *projects* that secure winning. Each project has four components to build alignment among the people who must execute for success:

1. **A champion**—one human being who has overall responsibility for delivering results.
2. **Deliverables**—clear end points that are quantified to the extent possible so team members know when they're having success.
3. **Timetable**—due dates for all deliverables.
4. **Budget**—broken down by dates and deliverables.

The final step on the alignment triangle is to measure and celebrate (that is, reward) interim progress—"Controls" in the VOSTC hierarchy you see on page 63.

Many companies inadvertently create alignment problems with their incentive systems. I experienced this while leading Trammell Crow

Company in the 1980s. We were in the business of building, leasing, and managing commercial real estate. Our systems were aligned around this mission, and that included our compensation system. Everyone we hired at Trammell Crow was paid the same salary—$18,000 per year. (This was at a time when the average MBA graduate might earn $100,000 in a "hot" field like consulting or investment banking.) We were able to hire talented people with low salaries because they recognized they'd make most of their compensation on profits from the building projects they developed—the kind of pay system used in many industries that's colloquially known as "you eat what you kill," but which business-school types call "pay for performance."

In good times, this compensation system created great alignment between a company whose goals were to aggressively build, lease, and manage new buildings and the partners who did the daily blocking-and-tackling to accomplish our chief objective.

The problem came in the late 1980s, when property markets were overvalued and overbuilt and a correction seemed almost certain. I wanted our partners to dramatically slow (or even stop) the pace of development activity, and I argued for less development. But our compensation system continued to provide heavy incentives to keep developing. In the end, we made adjustments, but too slowly. Like turning a fleet of battleships around, it took too long and, ultimately, the company was sold to Coldwell Banker (CBRE Group); today, it is again a large developer with incentives far better aligned with its objectives. Had we aligned our control system with our objectives in a timely fashion, the Trammell Crow Company would, in my opinion, be a large, stand-alone development firm, the envy of the real estate development world.

Any lack of alignment—from *values* at the pinnacle to *metrics* at the bottom, measuring the results of the *tactics* applied to execute a *strategy* to achieve a clear *goal*—is like the ignition timing being off in an internal combustion engine. For maximum power, the spark plug must fire the fuel/air mixture when the piston reaches top dead center. If ignition timing is off, the engine misfires, rattles when idling, and fails to produce the expected acceleration, until metal shavings begin to appear in the oil as the engine is degraded.

The analogue in a business system is that of misalignment among the five key elements required to manage any enterprise, institution, or family. Understanding the relationship between values, objectives, strategy, tactics, and controls allows one to defuse conflict, assess pain points, and attack problems in the right order and in the right way. More than anything, it represents a tool for the entrepreneurial leader to keep everyone on the same page, reminding the entire team of how each of these supports and must be consistent with the other, allowing the leader to make changes, resist pressures, and keep the enterprise on course. In my experience, this simple alignment map is the best predictor of the success of an enterprise, including the rigor required to establish clarity around each of the five categories, from values to the controls that support them.

RECAP

▶ Know that companies will fail to achieve their missions without alignment and, in contrast, will often succeed almost effortlessly when everyone is on the same page and all behaviors are self-reinforcing.

▶ Use the VOSTC chart to answer core questions around each of the five topics and to find areas of misalignment.

▶ Correct misalignments unless they are over values. When values aren't aligned, someone must leave the organization.

CRAFTING A CULTURE

There's no formula for great company culture. The key is to just treat your staff the way you would like to be treated.

—Richard Branson

A s you've read, I became the first investor in Bonobos, the online apparel company founded by Brian Spaly and Andy Dunn. Bonobos was one of my favorite investments even before Andy achieved a good return for investors by selling the company to Walmart. That's largely because of its unwavering focus on customer delight, complete with customer service reps ("customer ninjas" in Bonobos's corporate lingo) who go to great lengths to make sure customers are satisfied.

In contrast with what happens when you call the customer service department at most retailers, when customers call a Bonobos ninja, they connect with a flesh-and-blood human empowered to actually help them. Bonobos ninjas are guided by a simple question: "What would I want if I were the customer?"

One day, one of those ninjas, Kelsey Nash, received an email from a customer that read: "I had a fire at my house and one of my favorite flannel shirts was damaged. Do you know of a way to repair or replace it? I see you don't have this shirt on the website anymore."

Kelsey wrote back: "We're happy to replace your shirt. I'm so sorry about the fire. Is everybody all right?" The customer responded: "Actually, everybody's fine, except our fourteen-year old dog, who was trapped in the house and died."

Kelsey went into ninja mode. He got online, found a picture of his customer's dog on his Instagram account, commissioned a painting, and sent it along with a couple of flannel shirts to his customer. Stunned, his customer responded: "I'm not an emotional guy, but with all that had happened, I cried when I saw the painting."

Later, recounting his experience, the customer reflected, "What [Kelsey] did wasn't necessary. . . . He just thought it was the right thing to do. The only thing I've put up on the wall of our new home so far is that painting. It's right above my desk, on the wall above the window. When I walk in the door every morning, it's the first thing I see."

Bonobos makes great clothes, but its culture makes great covenants with customers. That leads not only to great hires but also to customers who learn to trust ninjas. Bonobos is a great example of how a company gives employees a simple mission they can translate into operational decisions—and which, taken together, create a powerful culture inside the company . . . and a strong brand outside it.

Compared with business disciplines such as finance or managerial tasks such as hiring, culture can seem amorphous. Left to their own devices, entrepreneurial leaders will never arrive at work and find the word *culture* at the top of the morning's to-do list. I once asked an executive to share the essence of his company's culture with students in a business school class I was teaching. His response was that in his company "we don't need no stinkin' culture." He was wrong. Every company has one, and if the leader doesn't care about it, chances are the culture stinks.

Leaders are responsible for shaping the culture of their organization, whether they are building one from scratch at a start-up or trying to nudge an existing culture in a more positive direction at a long-established firm.

How to do that? Let's start by defining some terms.

Ed Schein, the emeritus MIT professor whose research helped define and spread the notion of corporate culture, defines it as "a pattern of shared basic assumptions learned by a group as it solves its problems." Schein says culture is often driven by artifacts, espoused beliefs and values (the kind that people talk about), and basic underlying assumptions (the kind that are so universally held there's no need to articulate them).[1]

There's a clearer, less academic description of culture that I tend to prefer: it's simply "the way we do things around here." Culture is shaped by both written policies and informal practice. It's affected by compensation and performance evaluation systems, but it's more directly driven by the way leaders behave, how people treat each other, the stories that are told and retold until they become part of company lore, and the kinds of behaviors that are tolerated or aren't.

Consider all the things that define a corporate culture that aren't in any employee handbook: Do people show up for meetings five minutes early or five minutes late? Do people routinely use profanity, or is that frowned upon? Do people dress formally or casually at the office? Do bosses email subordinates at 9:00 p.m. and expect an instant reply? Even office design and architecture can affect culture. The culture in companies where a CEO sits in a baronial corner office will be very different from the culture in ones in which the CEO occupies a cubicle among the rank and file, as is common at start-ups and tech companies.

Together, this mishmash of formal and informal practices combine to become a company's culture, which I sometimes describe as *the covenant between colleagues and coworkers*.

What's the payoff from making the effort to develop a great culture? The best companies design their cultures to produce a sustainable competitive advantage. One tangible result is retaining top talent. As Jim Goodnight, founder and CEO of SAS Institute, once put it: "Ninety-five percent of my assets drive out the gate every evening. It's my job to maintain a work environment that keeps those people coming back every morning."[2] Having a great culture helps him do that.

Goodnight's approach to culture is based on a simple recognition: most of his employees are knowledge workers whose innovative ideas are essential to keeping the company's software products ahead of competitors'. Goodnight believes the more freedom he gives employees and the better he treats them, the more likely they are to work hard and go the extra mile to help the company strengthen its products. SAS's approach—characterized by generous perks and amenities—also stems from that philosophy. When Goodnight was starting out as a young engineer, he worked at NASA on the Apollo project that sent the first astronauts to the moon. The hours were ridiculously long, and every time Goodnight wanted a cup of coffee to keep himself alert, he had to pay for it. "This didn't make any sense to him," recalls Jenn Mann, SAS's human resources VP. "So when he started SAS, he made sure coffee and other beverages were provided in all cafes and in every break room on campus so our employees could get a drink whenever they wanted . . . for free."[3]

Entrepreneurial leaders recognize that they can't build a great culture all by themselves, so smart ones bring on a strong team member who will make that a core responsibility. Reed Hastings, the founder of Netflix, had such a partner in HR chief Patty McCord during the company's first decade. Together, Hastings and McCord built an unusual culture of transparency and accountability.

For instance, one of their principles is "Hire only fully formed adults," and then avoid overregulating them as if they were schoolchildren. Netflix pioneered the practice of giving employees unlimited vacation days (employees work it out with their managers), and its expense account policy consists of just five words: "Act in Netflix's best interests." McCord writes: "If you're careful to hire people who will put the company's interests first, who understand and support the desire for a high-performance workplace, 97 percent of your employees will do the right thing. Most companies spend endless time and money writing and enforcing HR policies to deal with problems the other 3 percent might cause. Instead, we tried really hard not to hire those people, and we let them go if it turned out we'd made a hiring mistake."[4] Hastings and McCord encapsulated their thinking about culture in a slide deck that went viral and has been viewed more than five million times.[5]

Cultures can be crafted in dramatically different ways, depending on what it will take to protect the firm's competitive strategy. In contrast to SAS, consider Walmart, whose strategy focuses on offering customers low prices. In order to maintain that edge, the company must keep its expenses down. If you spend time at Walmart headquarters in Bentonville, Arkansas, this defining element of its culture is obvious. Its offices and furnishings are economical. Its executives work *hard*, attending company meetings on Saturday mornings. When traveling on business, executives share hotel rooms to reduce travel expenses. The company's advertising tagline is "Save money. Live better." And even as Walmart approaches its seventh decade in business, "saving money" remains at the heart of how its employees operate every day. Low cost is embedded in its culture.

When an entrepreneurial leader thinks about crafting a culture, he or she must consider two things: the *type* of culture the company would most benefit from having and the *tools* he or she will use to drive the culture in that direction.

Leaders often use simple adjectives to describe a corporate culture: high-performing or collaborative or innovative. In my work with companies, the three adjectives I most often use when describing the culture I hope to craft are trusting, accountable, and respectful. Trust manifests in a range of ways, but very often it's evident when leaders give team members the power to carry out assignments and tasks, and to make decisions, without too much supervision. Accountability is a necessary condition for that kind of trust: if employees are given the freedom to work when and how they want and to make important decisions, they must recognize the implicit and reciprocal obligation that they will produce good results. Leaders support a culture of accountability by being clear about expectations and then ensuring negative consequences for those who miss deadlines, fail to meet a budget, or don't execute on the plan as they'd agreed to. In a respectful culture, people treat each other with kindness and caring no matter what's going on in the business.

Too many businesses suffer from a *toxic culture*—the kind that makes people dread going to work each day. There are many attributes that can be symptomatic of a toxic culture. Workplaces with toxic cultures tend to be settings where people don't trust each other, aren't held accountable to each other, and don't treat one another with respect. Emphasizing the three adjectives I put at the heart of culture will help to reduce the risk of toxicity.

When it comes to the tools leaders use to shape culture, the one I wield most frequently is what many call *hero stories*. Hero stories provide specific examples of people who've acted in line (or beyond expectations) in regard to cultural expectations. Celebrating real-life, specific stories serves several functions. It rewards the employee at the center of the story for above-the-call-of-duty behavior. It provides both a model and an incentive for other employees, who will want to mimic the action and perhaps be singled out as a future hero. In my role as board chairman or lead director, I sometimes open board meetings by reading letters from customers containing specific stories of exceptional service; doing this singles out our company's heroes and reminds everyone present that their behavior is at the center of our mission.

As a leader, I collect such tales. The Bonobos ninja who commissioned the dog painting is one. At JetBlue, my favorite involves a flight attendant working an early February flight. After the plane landed and the passengers disembarked, the crew began its usual procedure of cleaning out the airplane. When she was halfway through the plane, she looked in a seat-back pocket and made a surprising discovery: tickets to the Super Bowl, being held two days later. She instantly recognized that a passenger who's lost Super Bowl tickets is facing a full-blown crisis, so she got to work. She identified who'd been sitting in the seats, retrieved their contact information from customer service, and tried to contact them. When she learned they had already traveled to their hotel, which was more than thirty miles away, the flight attendant rented a car and hand-delivered the tickets to the passenger. This is the kind of service we should all aspire to give—which is why this is a hero story worth retelling.

Smart leaders make a regular practice of this. When new employees join JetBlue, many of them spend their first few days in Orlando at a new-employee training session. Before they receive training on the nuts-and-bolts tasks they will perform on the job, they spend time listening to senior JetBlue executives tell some of their own hero stories. We want these new employees (called Baby Blues in our culture) to begin "drinking the blue juice"—a phrase describing their immersion and acclimation to our JetBlue culture, which puts customer service above all else.[6]

Even as JetBlue approaches the twentieth anniversary of its first flight, we recognize how a culture that prioritizes above-expectations service is crucial to our success. Back when we launched the airline, we immediately began winning J.D. Power awards, proof that customers loved flying the airline. But when we parsed those scores, we found out they were mostly a function of our new aircraft, free live DirecTV, wide leather seats, and free snacks. Over time, those are elements that competitors can mimic. But if we can create and sustain a culture that prizes customer service, competitors will be hard pressed to match it. Research shows the average flight attendant has seven thousand interactions with passengers each month. We want every one of them to make the customer feel special—whether he's lost Super Bowl tickets in the seat-back pocket or she is nervously facing her first flight.

Beyond celebrating its heroes, companies must take other steps to support employees who uphold key values. When the Bonobos ninja commissioned a painting for a customer, that cost money—and so did renting the car to hand-deliver the JetBlue customers' football tickets. In a customer-first culture, employees are empowered to spend nominal sums (or issue refunds) without elaborate approvals from supervisors. Celebrating heroism isn't enough—company policies must provide flexibility and support for tomorrow's heroes to have the latitude they need to mimic these kinds of actions.

Sometimes totems, physical objects, or artifacts can be important drivers of culture too. At Peterson Partners, the investment fund I founded in Salt Lake City, we used to decorate our office with artwork. The paintings were pleasant to look at, but they weren't supporting or reinforcing the mission or culture of the firm. So we removed the art and replaced it with photos of the entrepreneurs in whom we were investing and the products and companies they were building. Now when our team walks the hallways, we are surrounded by subtle reminders that our primary role is to support and celebrate the people in whom we invest.

Back in the 1980s at Trammell Crow Company, I launched a program to get partners focused on making every division "shipshape," which meant focusing on profitability and capital structure. To reinforce that message, I hired an artisan who took partners' business cards and made them into sails for miniature 1800s-style sailing ships that went inside glass bottles. In the 2000s, Trammell Crow was purchased by CBRE Group, which is the world's largest commercial real estate services firm; today it is run by CEO Bob Sulentic, whom we hired at Trammell Crow Company many years ago. When I talked to Bob recently, he recalled that he still has the ship-in-the-bottle totem we used to highlight the shipshape program at Trammell Crow Company. "In business, you get a lot of mementos, and I rarely keep any of them," Bob says. "But even thirty years later, I still have that ship on display in my home, and I'm sure many of the other former Trammell Crow partners do too."[7]

There's one additional thing leaders can do to shape the culture—arguably the most important one. It's getting the right people into the company and getting the wrong ones out. (Sports fans call this latter move "addition by subtraction.") This is such an important part of what an entrepreneurial leader does that the entire next section of this book focuses on it. To learn more about this crucial strategy for building a great culture, read on.

RECAP

▶ Consider culture a valuable off-balance-sheet asset that—unlike products or delivery systems—cannot easily be copied by competitors.

▶ Invest in culture by rewarding those who behave consistently with it and coaching or removing those who violate it.

▶ Collect and recount hero stories that illustrate the most important elements of culture, recognizing and rewarding culture carriers.

SECURE
A TEAM

Teams succeed and fail together. An entrepreneurial leader empowers team members, reflects credit onto colleagues, and recognizes that business leadership is a team sport—one in which team chemistry matters. Nothing is more important to the entrepreneurial leader than ensuring the right people are on the field in the right positions. This means knowing how to find, recruit, interview, onboard, coach, assign, reassign, and, when necessary, remove those who reduce the team's likelihood of achieving its mission.

STEP 1

HIRING
GREAT PEOPLE

No one can whistle a symphony.

—Adage

This is the longest chapter in this book—for good reason. The best way to improve the performance of your team is to make the right choices when adding or replacing its members. An entrepreneurial leader's best decisions are her "great hires"; her worst decisions, "bad hires." The people you hire impact every part of your organization from its values and vision to its ability to innovate, adapt, and survive.

The wrong people don't fit at all—no matter their on-paper skills. They gum up the works—no matter their training or experience. And they damage the culture—no matter their other attributes. The right ones bring a special harmony to the way things run. They come up with new ideas and invent ways to improve the business. Like a great investment, they pay off at a multiple of expectations.

In *Good to Great*, Jim Collins argues that people are even more important than strategy. I agree. He wrote: "The executives who ignited the transformations from good to great did not first figure out where to drive the bus and then get people to take it there. No, they *first* got the right people on the bus (and the wrong people off the bus) and *then* figured out where to drive it. They said, in essence, 'Look, I don't really know where we should take this bus. But I know this much: If we get the right people on the bus, the right people in the right seats, and the wrong people off the bus, then we'll figure out how to take it someplace great.'"[1]

Like finding a great investment, finding a great person takes diligence and some degree of luck. It means locating the best candidates, interviewing them carefully, doing in-depth reference checks, and coaching them well once they're on board. And it means finding people who are excited about the mission of the enterprise.

When I begin looking to fill a job opening, I begin with self-talk, to put myself in the right mind-set for hiring. I tell myself: *It's a privilege to meet people who want to work with me. I'm looking for someone to work with for the next ten years. I will find someone with whom I can develop mutual trust.*

I also keep in mind the common pitfalls I have observed (and sometimes have made) when trying to identify and hire the best people. Here are the most common mistakes:

MISTAKE #1: HIRING YOURSELF (OVER AND OVER)

Managers love to select candidates who look and act like they do—people who went to the same school, or worked for the same prior employer, or have the same hobbies. There's plenty of research to show that similarities in experience, attitude, political views, and physical appearance all increase the likelihood that people "connect"—even if those similarities are hiding weaknesses that make the person ill suited for the job. No manager is immune from feeling comfortable with the familiar. For one thing, it's natural to like people who affirm our opinions and decisions. And we tend to communicate more easily with people who share our background, language, and beliefs. Better communication means fewer conflicts, and if we feel that we're going to get along with one person better than another, that's hard to resist.

Beware of this impulse. At the worst, an unchecked tendency to hire people just like you can be discriminatory—and beyond the legal risk, it's just unwise. More important, building a homogeneous organization will deprive you of the variety of perspectives, backgrounds, and skills that are invaluable when you're up against big problems or presented with big opportunities.

You want to work with a group of people who push each other beyond perceived limitations. Disparate backgrounds may help with innovation, testing biases, and ventilating possibilities—but only if people share a common objective.

MISTAKE #2: HIRING THE RÉSUMÉ, NOT THE PERSON

Hiring someone because they have an impressive résumé is like buying a car because you love the brochure. If you fail to look under the hood, your new hire may end up like the Fisker Karma, the coveted hybrid sports car that looked like a million bucks but was so riddled with glitches that the manufacturer went bankrupt.

Avoid lemons when hiring too. That means treating the résumé like an advertisement—good for basic information, but not the whole story. A candidate's education, skill set, and experience will be the first things to catch your eye. And, of course, it's also important to know whom the person has worked for, which technologies she knows, and how many people she's managed.

But what you're really selecting for are qualities you won't find on a résumé—brains and heart. They're at the root of a person's ability to confront unexpected challenges, to demonstrate wisdom and judgment, and to develop into an invaluable part of your team.

Brains implies more than a person's raw mental horsepower. One version of intelligence consists of having a flexible mind-set that combines book smarts and street smarts. That blend enables a person to navigate unfamiliar situations and make sense of many conflicting signals. (See Carol Dweck's book *Mindset* for a description of a "growth mind-set"). Can this person tell a good risk from a bad one? Can he absorb knowledge fast and apply it in real time? Does he have the social intelligence to work well with people around him? Will he learn from mistakes?

Heart is shorthand for the entire constellation of a candidate's values. It's the system of ethics and beliefs from which all choices and actions arise. Does he dive into whatever he's working on? Can he deal with tough setbacks? Take responsibility and share credit? Make things happen at critical moments, even when tired?

When you find a top-quality hire, you'll see that the answer to these questions is inevitably yes. Still, when deadlines loom, there's a temptation to snap up a skilled person whose résumé suggests she can help get your current product out the door. But be wary about striking a Faustian bargain: you may be trading a short-term fix for a long-term headache.

Caught up in day-to-day pressures, managers tend to downplay old-fashioned notions like character in favor of technical or functional skills that can help with short-term productivity. This is especially true in technical companies, and in cases when there are time pressures and an unfilled opening in the org chart. When there are no other employees who can step in and fill a role, technical capabilities take primacy. Character and other broad capabilities seem more like "nice to have's" rather than "essentials." In these situations, hiring managers develop a sort of tunnel vision, focusing on immediate needs and forgetting that skills don't arrive without a person wrapped around them.

While technical expertise may be the price of admission if you're dealing with surgery, engine repair, or laboratory research, it is often not the critical determinant of whether someone will be an exceptional performer as a manager or leader. Indeed, in a team setting, most people are hired for what they know and fired for how they apply what they know.

Whenever I've relegated brains and heart to a secondary priority, over time, my shortsightedness has turned out to be a recipe for disappointment. While specific skills may loom large in the short term, a person's character and ability to figure out the unexpected determine performance over the long term. If I had to choose one over the other, I would go with brains (raw capacity, curiosity, the ability to learn) and heart (character, drive, integrity) and figure that a person who possesses them will be able to acquire any skills needed to get the job done.

MISTAKE #3: FAILING TO DO IN-DEPTH INTERVIEWS

Many managers don't know how to conduct in-depth interviews, which are first and foremost fact-finding missions. Their purpose is to collect specific details about a candidate's accomplishments and to reveal shortcomings that may prevent hiring mistakes.

Many interviews are entered into with little preparation, are not pursued with the kind of structure that completes a picture, and conclude too quickly. In many instances, candidates are rushed from interviewer to interviewer, each armed only with a résumé he was handed that morning. Furthermore, the interviewing team often has no clear strategy for what each is trying to discover. Without a plan, they cruise through conversations on autopilot, asking predictable questions and getting canned answers: Where do you see yourself in five years? Which project have you enjoyed working on most? What do you see as your main strengths and weaknesses?

Because interviews tend to be short—generally thirty to sixty minutes—they stay at a fairly superficial level. Whether they realize it or not, most interviewers are mostly assessing likeability. By contrast, one of the most successful placement firms I know conducts four-hour interviews that go through a lifetime of experience and decision making.

One of the best interview techniques involves listening carefully to questions the candidate asks, then asking yourself: What is this person looking to get out of the job? What are her concerns? What does "winning" look like for her? Because you can't make a great hire unless the candidate makes a great decision, too, it is vital to ask yourself if you are also a fit for her. You, too, should expect to be interviewed by qualified candidates. Your insightful descriptions of the strengths and limitations of the organization will help the candidate make a wise determination—a vital part of the hiring equation.

Be sure to ask the candidate what prior supervisors will tell you when you call. The specter of a reference check not only keeps interviewees honest, but it also gives you insight into how self-aware they are.

And when you're done, pull the interviewing team together right away to compare notes. Insights are freshest on the same day. If you're too busy to do this right, you'll find you'll be even busier later when you have to replace the new hire and repeat the process.

MISTAKE #4: LAZY REFERENCE CHECKING

There are several slipups that people make when reference checking. The most obvious is failing to do the check at all. When managers fail to check references, it is typically because they don't believe reference checks yield useful information. But this is because they don't do them well.

A common mistake is relying solely on primary references (those provided directly by the candidate) and failing to follow up with secondary references. Primary references tend to be predictable, which explains why many managers don't bother checking them. By contrast, secondary references can provide valuable perspectives on a candidate's qualifications and additional facts about a person's performance and character. They can be obtained by asking primary references to identify other people familiar with a candidate's work, by asking the candidate to provide other references, or by networking.

Reference calls are not a "check the box" hiring chore to get quickly off your list. And they should not be delegated. You may get help verifying references' positions, histories, and employment dates, but you should do the reference check yourself, if the hire is for your team.

Positively phrased questions like "What is his biggest opportunity to improve?" can help with getting insights. Less usual questions, such as "What type of job would you not hire this person for?" or "How does this person choose between competing priorities?" can give a sense of values. Encourage disclosure with open-ended questions: "Is there anything else I should know when considering him for the job?" Finally, remember that the more natural the conversation, the more likely the reference is to be helpful. And be sure to thank references and to assure them of confidentiality.

With great people, you can dig pretty far into their network and have a hard time finding colleagues who didn't like working with them. It's the opposite with candidates you want to avoid—you may only have to spend twenty minutes on the phone before you think: "Next!"

Finally, if you plan to look beyond the list of references the candidate gives you, you need to let him or her know in advance that you'll be doing so. That'll give him an opportunity to tell you if there are people or places he'd prefer you not contact, and why. If someone refuses to let you talk with anyone but a couple of prewired references, you might wonder if there's something going on.

MISTAKE #5: FREEZING OUT YOUR TEAM

Managers should generally involve members of the team in the hiring process. These may include people who will be working directly with the new hire, people familiar with the job and its requirements, and those to whom the new hire will be accountable.

By excluding the internal team from the hiring process, you're saying you don't trust them. By failing to involve them, you may not only miss out on subtle details but also miss the opportunity to recruit their support. If they become resentful or threatened, you may inadvertently set up your new hire for failure. However, don't relinquish the role of making the final call. Involving the team doesn't mean everyone gets a vote. After all, you'll be ultimately responsible for the team's output.

MISTAKE #6: OVERRELYING ON INTERNAL
OR EXTERNAL CANDIDATES

You don't want to go outside for every important hire, nor do you want to confine yourself to internal candidates. Each approach has its advantages—but either can become a liability if you rely on it too much.

Organizations often feel they need to go outside to find the best candidates. But this has two downsides. First, it suggests to employees that they are not valued by sending a message that internal candidates are simply not strong enough to take on additional responsibilities. Second, it can be demotivating, because it limits opportunities for upward mobility. This often leads to retention problems.

Entrepreneurial leaders recognize that there are often enormous benefits to selecting internal candidates. For one thing, far more is known about their character and their capabilities. Less is left to chance. Hiring from within also sends an encouraging message to the rest of the organization that employees are valued for their contributions and that the firm wants to develop them. Finally, sending an internal-candidates-will-be-considered message and giving insiders a first look may help employees be more supportive when it does prove necessary to bring in talent from outside.

On the other hand, outside hires can bring skills, ideas, and experience that people on the home team just don't have. If your culture needs repair, new hires are invaluable. Inside-only hiring can lead to insularity and weaken your ability to innovate. Worse, in a rapidly evolving industry, you can risk falling out of touch with your customers and the market.

When you're trying to decide whether to hire an internal or external candidate, interview both. For internal candidates who don't make the cut, it's an opportunity to offer feedback and help craft a plan to improve and advance. Likewise, if you decide to go with an insider, having talked to external candidates will give you insight into what's happening in the industry, to meet candidates who may be a good fit for later, and to feel greater confidence in your internal candidate.

In the long run, you'll want to strike a balance between keeping current employees engaged and excited and bringing in fresh talent and perspective.

MISTAKE #7: MAKING IT ALL ABOUT THE MONEY

When deciding what to pay your new hires, get it right. Pay too little, and they will quickly become dissatisfied and/or resentful—and quit for a better opportunity. Pay too much, and they'll be happy for a while—but soon may feel they've traded away their freedom for financial security. Mortgages, car payments, and school tuitions may lock them into jobs they can't stand, or no longer do well. They'll want to leave but can't afford to. Most managers recognize the former risk; too few understand the latter.

Organizations made up of people who chose their jobs based on the highest salaries are miserable places to work—full of petty jealousies and politics, and hostile to new hires. Anyone who does business with Wall Street firms, which sometime lure recruits with outrageous salary and bonus packages, will recognize this phenomenon.

Instead, your hiring goal should be to create an all-volunteer organization, where everyone is there because they want to be. Many of today's knowledge workers are flexible enough to migrate between jobs if they're feeling unappreciated or underpaid. Remember, your competitors are just around the corner: there will always be a rival willing to pay "above market" to hire away your best people.

Instead of making it all about the paycheck, entrepreneurial leaders help team members find meaning in their jobs and feel invested in the purpose of the organization by using specific tools: access to senior management, titles, public credit when projects go well, and learning opportunities, whether through formal programs or informal mentorship.

People who prefer money to these other kinds of compensation may be "coin-operated," the kind of people who hang around only until a better-paying gig comes along. But the people who thrive in an environment that prizes respect and opportunity are likely to stay, to be more invested in their work, and to create value for themselves and the organization—all things that money can't buy.

MISTAKE #8: NOT ONBOARDING PROPERLY

A successful hire doesn't end with a job offer and a handshake. "Welcome aboard" is just the beginning. New employees must be socialized and integrated into the organization. The first ninety days of a new employee's tenure is a critical period.

When I hire someone, I start by making the new employee's success an explicit personal goal. By the end of ninety days, I want the team to wonder how they got along before the new person joined, I want the new employee to marvel at how much she enjoys the job—and as the manager, I want to be excited about how much the new employee might develop and contribute in the future.

Managers should make clear that the entire team is responsible for onboarding. Just as the human body can reject a transplanted organ, existing teams can be hostile to new members without the right groundwork. Getting your team involved in the hiring process is a good start, but don't stop there. Ask the team for thoughts about how to make the new person feel welcome, perhaps something that helped them in their early days on the job. Just reminding the team about first-day anxiety will communicate a level of care that can pay dividends.

When the new employee does something right or wrong, provide frank, real-time feedback. Likewise, tell her that you want to hear her unvarnished perspective on the way you work—so the feedback goes both ways.

Managers should also demonstrate behavior, not just talk about it. It's easy to rattle off a list of virtues when you're describing what your organization is all about. But you can't teach your employees virtues by reading them from the handbook. Your organization's values come from where it spends its time, money, and energy—and perhaps more than that, how its people act and the choices they make.

Even if you avoid these common missteps, eventually you're going to make a bad hire. Instead of beating yourself up about it, find a way to gracefully undo the mistake.

You'll usually know something's wrong in the first ninety days. The new person will be late completing projects, won't have the skills you might have thought, or won't seem to be putting in a lot of effort. Maybe he doesn't really get along with—or "get"—the team. It's less what he does than how he does it.

The longer you keep the wrong person on, the worse the mistake becomes. Problems compound as the recruit's performance puts more demands on the people around him.

You'll never have a perfect hiring batting average, but if you ignore your own mistakes and hope they go away, you'll be doing a major disservice both to your organization and to the person you've hired. Put yourself in his shoes: if your new boss was certain you weren't the right person for the job, would you want her to tell you or to pretend everything was okay? It's always best to face mistakes squarely, do your best to address them, and move forward.

The good news is that, as in many of life's most important activities, there's an experience curve when it comes to hiring. If you do it often, avoid the common mistakes, and try to learn from the ones you do make, you will get better over time. And the better you get, the stronger your team will become.

RECAP

▶ Consider the process of writing the job description, sourcing candidates, interviewing them, onboarding new hires, giving assignments and feedback, reassignments, and coaching your most important jobs as an entrepreneurial leader.

▶ Learn from your mistakes. No one gets hiring right all the time. Figure out the pattern of your missteps and make adjustments.

▶ Hire for values consistency, an ability to work well with others, and specific skills—in that order.

DEMONSTRATING EFFECTIVE ATTITUDES

Courage and perseverance have a magical talisman,
before which difficulties disappear and obstacles vanish
into air.

—John Quincy Adams

n April 2011, when Stanford's Graduate School of Business opened its new $345 million campus, it wanted to enliven its opening ceremony with something more than bland ribbon cuttings and speeches. So the dean asked a tenured colleague, Jeff Pfeffer, and me, an adjunct professor, to appear before a large audience for an on-stage debate, under the title "What It Takes to Get to the Top."

For many years, Pfeffer, who is the leading scholar on issues of power, had been teaching a popular course called "Paths to Power." He'd summarized its lessons in his 2010 book *Power: Why Some People Have It and Some People Don't*. In the book, he explains why succeeding in business requires a ruthless self-interest, a disregard for the well-being of others, the routine use of fear and bullying tactics, and the pursuit of power not only as a means but as an end in itself. In Pfeffer's view, there's no disputing the wisdom that nice guys finish last.

Not surprisingly, I view the world 180 degrees differently. Here's how *Bloomberg* described the debate: "It took place in front of a packed auditorium in which Peterson argued that 'trust and respect for others are essential in leadership; intimidation and manipulation always fail in the end.' Pfeffer argued, on the other hand, the core thesis of his leadership research: 'The odds are you can't be nice, honest, fair, and also successful; the path to power is paved with ruthless self-promotion.'"[1]

At the debate, I told Pfeffer I wished we could set up an experiment. We'd each be given one hundred pairs of identical companies to run, we'd lead them using our own very different styles, and after some period of time, we'd revisit them to see which had performed better. At the event, I told him I was confident I'd beat him ninety-nine times out of one hundred. A few weeks later, I reached out to amend the bet, joking that I'd beat him one hundred times out of one hundred. While offered as a good-natured jab, I'm convinced of it.

At root, Pfeffer and I disagree about what kind of attitude it takes to succeed as a leader. By attitude, I refer to everyday behavior and demeanor, the emotions you project, how you interact with people, and the way you carry yourself. Do you behave in a way that encourages others to trust you? To respect you? Do you project the right blend of confidence and humility? And can you carry yourself as a leader honestly and authentically without having to resort to power plays?

I have seen many leaders who demonstrate the right attitude—but I have also seen how the wrong attitude can limit an executive's success. Many years ago, when I was leading Trammell Crow Company, I needed to hire a functional specialist for a C-suite role. I knew a guy who'd worked with us on some deals, and I felt I'd gotten to know him well. He was phenomenally smart, and like many people, I'm a sucker for a high IQ. We hired him—and it soon became clear that we had a problem that only grew worse.

Real estate executives are street-smart and instinctive. This executive, who exuded an exceptional technical intelligence, didn't respect their brand of intelligence, so his demeanor in interactions with colleagues was condescending. In most meetings, he was almost certainly the proverbial smartest guy in the room—but acting as if that were true was off-putting to his new colleagues. And since he'd come from a professional services firm where young associates work extremely long hours, his expectations for his new staff—and the manner in which he issued commands to them—came as a shock. A year into his new role, I conducted a 360-degree review, and we met to go over the results. I confirmed how much I liked him and valued his work, but then I handed him a single sheet summarizing what his new colleagues thought of him. Reading it, his eyes began to water. "I had no idea," he said. He immediately recognized that he'd need to leave, and he was right. When I recall this experience, the takeaway is that someone with a high IQ but the wrong attitude will have a hard time succeeding.

Like Pfeffer, many people believe in the "nice guys finish last" leadership hypothesis. I don't. Based on decades of working with flesh-and-blood entrepreneurial leaders, I'm convinced that their success may depend as much on their attitude as on any other single factor. When we evaluate leaders, we tend to focus on what they do—the substantive decisions on issues of strategy, talent development, and big product bets—as determinants of organizational success. Substance counts, but style does too—style referring not to *what* they do but *how* they do it.

When I meet entrepreneurial leaders, I'm often struck by their optimism, energy, and even-keeled temperament. Successful entrepreneurial leaders—whether early- or later-stage leaders—can be found at either side of the continua below (but in my experience, many more are found on the left):

SELF-TALK

Optimistic ←——————→	Pessimistic
Other-centric ←——————→	Egocentric
Big picture ←——————→	Small picture
Abundance (½ full) ←——————→	Scarcity (½ empty)
Trusting ←——————→	Wary
Empowering ←——————→	Power hoarding
Risk taking ←——————→	Cautious
Failure okay ←——————→	Failure shameful
Flexible ←——————→	Fixed

In trying to clearly define what I mean by the most effective demeanor, I've learned to focus on five elements of spirit, or character traits, possessed (or developed) by those most likely to inspire others to create durable change and lasting institutions.

Likable: In grade school, people know it's important to be liked, but when they enter the business world, sometimes they forget the importance of this simple dynamic. Deepak Malhotra, who teaches negotiation at Harvard Business School, emphasizes this when advising students and others on how to negotiate their job offers. In a list of fifteen things to remember, his first point is: don't underestimate the importance of likability. "People are going to fight for you only if they like you," Malhotra writes. "Anything you do in a negotiation that makes you less likable reduces the chances that the other side will work to get you a better offer."[2] This is true in most areas of business—not only negotiation.

The importance of likability is not a new insight. "Even in such technical [work] as engineering, about 15 percent of one's financial success is due to one's technical knowledge and about 85 percent is due to skill in human engineering—to having the personality and ability to lead people," Dale Carnegie wrote in his 1936 classic *How to Win Friends and Influence People*.[3] The world has changed dramatically since Carnegie wrote those words—but the advice hasn't.

Grateful: Gratitude is infectious. It leads to optimism, resilience, and a virtuous cycle that prompts others to kindness, respect, and generosity. People wired for gratitude spread good cheer.

Some of the traits on this list may seem inborn, or difficult to cultivate. Gratitude is not. Martin Seligman, the University of Pennsylvania psychology professor and founder of the positive psychology movement, suggests two exercises that can make anyone both feel more gratitude and make their gratitude more apparent to others. The first exercise, which he calls a *gratitude visit*, consists of writing a letter to someone from your past who said or did something that changed your life in a positive way. "The letter should be concrete and about three hundred words: be specific about what she did for you and how it affected your life," Seligman writes.[4] Then get in touch with the person and make an appointment to deliver it in person, reading it aloud and noting the recipient's reactions. The second exercise is called *three blessings*. "We think too much about what goes wrong and not enough about what goes right in our lives," Seligman writes, explaining how evolution may have rewarded people who try to learn from bad events to increase their odds of survival. To overcome this natural tendency, Seligman suggests that each night, people write down three events of that day for which they were grateful. "Writing about why the positive events in your life happened may seem awkward at first, but please stick with it for one week," he says. "It will get easier. The odds are that you will be less depressed, happier, and addicted to this exercise six months from now."[5]

Happy: The happiest people are not merely cheerful; they are joyful. They don't waste time in comparisons that put constant pressure on the organization to make sure everything is trued up at every instant. (As the adage goes, "Comparison is the thief of joy.") Unhappy people carry an inconsolable bitterness that is an organizational cancer. I've seen cultures heal simply by encouraging those who are unhappy to be miserable elsewhere.

Admittedly, *happy* may seem incongruous with *demanding* or *hard-charging*—adjectives more typically used to describe high-performing leaders. But over many years, I've observed in myself and others that nice, happy, and kind can lead to a different kind of high performance—one in which team members feel valued and content. One observer went so far as to compare my leadership style to that of the children's TV host Mr. Rogers. Describing a lecture I gave at Stanford, he wrote: "Peterson's [lecture] sounded to me like the thematic backbeat for a Mr. Rogers episode: 'You're in charge of yourself, and you get to decide who you want to be. Other people matter a lot, so take time to care for and be kind to them. Work hard at something that's meaningful to you. Tell the truth. And bear in mind that your reputation follows you everywhere.'"[6] That's a great summary, to which I'd only add: be happy in your day-to-day work life—and if you're not, find something else to do.

Humble: Humility allows people to learn from mistakes, to embrace feedback, to grow with new information. Humble leaders create the kind of learning organization described by MIT's Peter Senge in his book *The Fifth*

Discipline. By recognizing their own fallibility and the necessity of learning from mistakes, they mobilize teams to behave in the same way, recognizing shortcomings not as a weakness but as an opportunity to improve.

Nitin Nohria, dean of Harvard Business School, has created a taxonomy of different kinds of humility. *Intellectual humility* recognizes that no matter how much you've achieved, there are likely others smarter than you. *Moral humility* recognizes that "no matter how self-assured you are about your moral compass, you are vulnerable, under stress or in certain contexts, to losing your way," he has said. *Personal humility* means acting with modesty and living simply. Nohria says: "No matter what you accomplish, always remain humble."[7]

Humorous: Team members who are funny lighten burdens and make work fun. Self-deprecating humor—particularly from leaders unafraid of laughing at their foibles—comes not from self-doubt but from self-confidence. It communicates one's humility. This trait also creates a safety valve on pressure and stress.

Data collected by Stanford professor Jennifer Aaker and lecturer Naomi Bagdonas suggest that people fall off a "humor cliff" when entering the workforce—they become fearful of making a joke.[8] That's a mistake. I've made it through any number of tense moments with a little humor—never a canned joke or a crack that comes at the expense of another but instead a certain lightheartedness or self-deprecation. I've found that gently mocking my own shortcomings helps to connect with others. I figure the team all knows my limits anyway, so why pretend otherwise? Humor can also render memorable what is otherwise tedious. At a physiological level, a bit of levity, good-natured ribbing, and thoughtful celebration releases the oxytocin and dopamine that help with memory and information processing. I'm not alone in appreciating this measure of spirit. A survey of more than seven hundred CEOs by Hodge-Cronin and Associates showed that 98 percent of CEOs prefer job candidates with a sense of humor.[9]

In 1964, Norman Cousins, editor of the *Saturday Review*, was diagnosed with ankylosing spondylitis, a rare disease of the connective tissues. He was given only a few months to live and a one-in-five-hundred chance of recovery.[10] A journalist by training, Cousins did a lot of research, and made three decisions about his treatment. First, he changed his environs: he fired his doctor, left the hospital, and checked into a hotel. He took massive doses of Vitamin C intravenously. Finally, he started laughing aloud by watching funny movies and television shows—whatever he could find to take his mind off his unrelenting pain. Cousins lived for another twenty-six years—and claimed, with some evidence, that he'd laughed his way back to health.[11]

Of course, not every leader will be likable, grateful, happy, humble, and humorous. Some leaders are just plain jerks. Steve Jobs is probably the most-cited example of this—someone who berated subordinates, parked in handicapped parking spaces, and played fast and loose with the accounting for his stock options. His life presents an interesting hypothetical: Could he have succeeded (or be even better remembered) if he'd shown a softer, more civil side at work? Would his legacy shine brighter if Walter Isaacson's biography of him weren't filled with cringe-worthy stories of his behavior?

Compared with entrepreneurial leaders, presiders and managers are better able to survive and succeed despite deficiencies in these positive traits, because they are more reliant on power and less on trust.

RECAP

▶ People don't just listen to what is said. They are also highly attuned to what's behind actions and behaviors.

▶ If attitudes don't include likability, gratitude, happiness, humility, and humor, consider using the techniques discussed in Rewriting Your Operating System (p. 12) to increase these qualities.

▶ If you're going to implement change based on power, expect that change to be transitory—and expect a replacement to find that change hard to maintain.

STEP 3

HELPING PEOPLE IMPROVE

Criticism may not be agreeable, but it is necessary. It fulfills the same function as pain in the human body; it calls attention to an unhealthy state of things.

—Winston Churchill, interview,
New Statesman, January 7, 1939

When most people think about *coaching*, their minds immediately go to sports, which makes sense. Athletics is the environment where most of us first encounter a person called a coach whose feedback and advice are supposed to help us perform better.

I've learned a lot about coaching during my business career, but I've also learned a lot from my son-in-law Mark Harris.[1] Today Mark is a successful investor, but when he began dating my daughter, Sarah (whom he eventually married), he was a college football player—one who went on to spend four years with the San Francisco 49ers. You don't make it to the NFL without superb athletic skills, but looking back on his career, Mark gives most of the credit for his success to a series of gifted and caring coaches.

"I was never really highly recruited during any part of my career," Mark says. After high school, he briefly attended Southern Utah University before heading to Barcelona, Spain, for a two-year church mission. Upon his return, he won a football scholarship to Ricks College (now BYU–Idaho), whose team was coached by Ron Haun, a renowned junior college coach. Initially, Haun hadn't shown much interest in Mark (an assistant coach had recruited him). During practices, however, Mark played well enough to attract Haun's attention. One day Haun pulled him aside and promised to make him the focal point of the offense the following season. "It was a transformational moment in my career," Mark says. The next fall, the team was crowned the junior college national champion by *USA Today*. Mark was named an All-American, and he was recruited to finish his collegiate career at Stanford, where he played for the legendary coaches Bill Walsh and Tyrone Willingham. By the time Mark graduated from Stanford, Walsh was serving as a 49ers special assistant, and he suggested the San Francisco team sign Mark—so they did.

"I was the backup to two Hall of Fame receivers, Jerry Rice and Terrell Owens, so I didn't get a lot of reps in practice," Mark says. Nonetheless, over four seasons in the National Football League, he received near-constant feedback from receivers' coach Larry Kirksey, who became another role-model coach and helped shape Mark into who he is today. "Larry gave me time, he gave me attention, and he made me feel like I was an all-star," Mark says. "He made sure I was being mentored, I was being practiced, that I was being praised when I did things right. I would walk through fire for that guy. I think that's what all good coaches do in a way—you want to perform not because you fear them but because you respect them. I wanted to do well because of all the work Larry put into me and because I knew he wanted me to do well."

Since retiring from football in 1999, Mark has spent much of his time watching how the CEOs of his portfolio companies try to coach their own employees. Mark observes that the best leaders coach employees as a day-to-day part of being a good boss. "The best CEOs see coaching as a natural extension of their responsibilities—they're not consciously trying to coach," he says. "They're just trying to do their best to make the company successful."

In working to make their organization perform well, every entrepreneurial leader should do the same—and consider coaching a priority. This means finding joy in others' progress, celebrating it when it occurs, and giving feedback when it falls short.

Coaching mustn't be confused with a performance review. While the latter has its place, it's often used as part of a perfunctory, once-a-year salary review—or, done clumsily, as preamble to termination. (More on that in the next chapter.)

The real power of feedback comes with its frequency, timing, and elegance. I've learned to give feedback in the moment, inviting the same. There's far more power in immediate coaching than in awaiting a year-end report card.

Letting people know how they might do better is often uncomfortable for new leaders. Feedback can stir up self-doubt, defensiveness, and career worries—and, if handled poorly, can be radioactive. So get good at it. Make it fun, nonthreatening, two-way, and frequent. And know that it's not about pointing out another's weaknesses or mistakes. It's about helping them build on their strengths, celebrating as well as correcting. Finally, I've learned that it costs nothing to ask permission before giving feedback. It's always granted; and it shows a level of respect that makes it easier to take.

Since operating without feedback is like driving a car with no speedometer, learning to cook without tasting the food, or playing basketball without a scoreboard, don't try to lead without the tool of feedback. If done right, well-considered feedback makes everything more fun and everyone more productive. I often refer to feedback with the tagline for Wheaties cereal—it really is "the breakfast of champions."

Many emerging leaders have been on the receiving end of vague, unnecessarily negative feedback, with no clear plan for improvement. Because of this experience, they tend to perpetuate the recipe for demoralizing a team.

Done right, feedback can be transformative and redemptive. Here are a few guidelines:

- **Don't wing it.** The words you choose matter. Practice what you're going to say and how to say it. Consider rehearsing with a trusted partner. Your attitude, the accuracy of what you say, and the care with which you say it may matter as much as the specifics.

- **Lean positive.** Every time you offer feedback, some (if not most) of it should be positive. Look for opportunities to note successes even as you offer suggestions for improvement. Celebrating performance has a salutary effect and is much more powerful than pointing out shortcomings. Dispensing encouragement is infectious.

- **Be specific.** There's no point in telling someone he needs to be "more punctual" or "more diplomatic." Give examples and specific suggestions for improvement. Replace "You need to be more punctual" with "Let's keep track of what time we start our weekly staff meetings in the coming month and then talk about how it went."

- **Don't limit feedback to an annual event.** Encourage regular and informal assessment. Make a deal with your team to offer (and accept) real-time tweaks. Indeed, the best opportunities for this are when you catch yourselves in the moment—when you can reflect on a missed cue or a better way to handle a situation. Make talking about "how we're doing" a regular, easy and on-the-way-to-winning exchange.

- **Keep it cool.** Don't use high-velocity language. Labeling someone "lazy" or "inept" will invariably come back to bite you. That's also a mistake because good feedback focuses on behaviors, not character or personality flaws. And never shout, stand, or be animated. People will recall how *they* felt, not what you said—so cool it.

- **Don't deluge.** People can only process so many suggestions at once. If you have more than an item or two for someone to consider, create a general heading, like goal setting, cooperation, or communication, and offer an example with a specific suggestion for improvement.

- **If it's serious, say so.** Occasionally, you may need to let someone know that unless she makes specific changes, her job is in jeopardy. If so, be direct. Let her know if something is getting in the way of her professional development and could lead to dismissal if unaddressed. If this feedback is offered with a plan to follow up, it may light the fire that could lead to improvement. If the situation is this serious, consider putting the feedback and plan in writing. At the least, this approach sets up a later conversation that won't be a surprise.

- **Follow up.** By noting improvements on the spot, you'll reinforce that you're paying attention. Check in soon about any plan you made together. And as you notice efforts to improve, mention them. I have a rule as board chair (or lead director) not to leave town without sitting with the CEO to go over what independent directors talked about in executive session, the part of the meeting in which directors talk without the CEO in the room. I've learned that—unless I do this—CEOs assume the worst.

- **Consider return feedback a gift.** There are no percentages in giving a superior feedback about things to work on. In other words, there's plenty of risk and no direct reward to giving a boss feedback. It's safer to say nothing. So if a subordinate offers input, thank him and make a special effort to reward his risk taking.

- **Keep it confidential.** Feedback sessions are private. Don't ever share feedback with someone else. In giving feedback, you're seeking to help the person and the organization. Nothing good will come from sharing one person's issues with another.

The aim is to build a culture in which people feel confident about sharing feedback without fearing that it will be taken personally. Honest, thoughtful feedback can build trust, strengthen bonds, and generate progress. Done well, it's the breakfast of champions.

If you spend time around companies, you may be shocked by how little time bosses spend coaching and training their subordinates. "People at McDonald's get trained for their positions, but people with far more complicated jobs don't," the venture capitalist Ben Horowitz writes in *The Hard Thing About Hard Things*. "A lot of companies think their employees are so smart that they require no training. That's silly."[2] Ben is right—teaching employees how to do better is among every boss's first responsibilities.

Another striking thing about good coaching: successful people continue to seek it out, no matter what level they have reached. They also recognize and credit the key coaches (or bosses) who provided feedback and direction along the way. That's true for my former NFL son-in-law, and it's true for me too.

Within a few years of joining Trammell Crow Company, I was called back to headquarters to serve as its chief financial officer. Typically a CFO has a background in accounting and a CPA certification; I had neither. I knew I needed help. So I recruited the CPAs in the organization to coach me on how to understand and untangle the firm's accounts, speak the language required of a CFO, and fill in the gaps in my technical knowledge. In business we tend to think that coaching should come from one's immediate supervisor, but that's not necessarily the best approach. In my case, my boss was the CEO, who had neither the inclination nor the necessary technical knowledge to help coach me into the CFO role. So I pursued a more imaginative approach, and my junior coaches filled the gap.

When I became Trammell Crow's CEO in the late 1980s, I recognized I could use additional coaching to succeed in this new role. One of the challenges of the CEO job is that he or she reports to the board, not a single supervisor, so there's no built-in mechanism for a CEO to receive coaching. I was fortunate: someone in my network was a close friend of Bob Waterman, the former McKinsey consultant who'd coauthored *In Search of Excellence*, one of the most successful business books in publishing history. After an introduction, I told Bob I needed some coaching, and asked if he'd help. He graciously agreed.

Early in our work together, I asked Bob to attend a board meeting that I chaired. Knowing that my coach was in attendance, I made sure to bring my A-game that day. I was analytical, articulate, and persuasive. Although I didn't say so out loud, I honestly thought I'd done a brilliant job—and after the meeting wrapped up, I couldn't wait for my coaching session with Bob, where I was sure he'd tell me exactly that.

"What'd you think?" I asked him. Bob wasn't impressed. "You talk too much," he said simply. "Okay," I said, trying my best to react nondefensively. "But what did you think about the substance of the discussion?" He stared at me and said it again: "You talk too much."

This wasn't a minor point. In Bob's view, my analysis of the situation the board had been discussing was spot-on, but instead of taking the directors on a journey in which they all felt they'd contributed to the conclusion we reached as a group, I'd short-cut the process and preemptively announced the conclusion. By not coaxing sufficient participation from every member of the board, Bob felt I wasn't getting sufficient buy-in to the decision we'd made. Their lack of participation and buy-in would reduce the odds of successful execution.

McKinsey had trained Bob well. Within a couple of hours, he had successfully diagnosed the problem and given me a prescription to try to do better—which I did.

Mark Harris made it to the NFL because of great coaching, and I was more effective as a leader because of the coaching I received from Bob Waterman and others. Every entrepreneurial leader should do the same for the people on his or her team.

RECAP

▶ Learn to give—and to receive—regular feedback, embracing the ten feedback rules until they come naturally.

▶ Make feedback fun, a way to learn and to grow, never taking offense, always seeing it as information that can either be incorporated or ignored.

▶ Consider hiring a coach to help you gain the skills you need, just as if you were an elite athlete.

STEP 4

FIRING WITH EMPATHY

Treat [the person you're firing] the same way you'd want to be treated if you were in that situation. They're still a good person, just not the right fit. So how do you help them move on in a productive way that allows them to maintain their dignity?

—Mary Barra, CEO General Motors,
interview, *Esquire*, April 26, 2016

In 2007, after nearly a decade of spectacular growth, JetBlue began to struggle. A Valentine's Day ice storm at New York's Kennedy International Airport, a JetBlue hub, had stranded passengers. Hundreds of people were stuck in planes on the tarmac for hours. The episode revealed glaring weaknesses in our operating systems. In our boardroom, directors discussed not only the costly incident and its aftermath but the larger lessons we should draw from it.

Since its first flight in 2000, JetBlue had risen to become America's eighth-largest airline. Much of the credit for that goes to its visionary founder, David Neeleman. But in the months after the so-called Valentine's Day Massacre, directors slowly reached consensus that for all his brilliance as a company founder, Neeleman might no longer be the best person to serve as JetBlue's CEO going into its next chapter. Even though he'd started the company and remained its largest individual shareholder, it was time to do what managers must do with employees for whom the job is no longer a fit—replace him.

Since I was the lead director, I drew the short straw. Another director and I went to his office and told David, clearly and directly, that we'd decided to appoint a new CEO and briefly explained why. To soften the blow, we asked him to remain as chairman of the board. David was upset and said we were making a mistake. We listened to his protests but remained resolute and moved the discussion to next steps, including a public announcement of the leadership change.

More than a decade later, David remains upset about the board's decision. When I showed him the manuscript for this book prior to publication, David sent me a long email defending his actions and criticizing directors and his successor. It read, in part: "This is not to say that I didn't make mistakes running the company. I did, but those mistakes were fixable and were in the process of being fixed before I was fired. The board acted way too hastily."

Despite that, David and I have maintained a long-running professional relationship. I continue to consider him the greatest commercial airline entrepreneur of all time. I even personally invested in his launch of Azul, a low-cost airline based in Brazil, where he grew up.

Even the best leaders dread firing people. I lost sleep in the days surrounding Neeleman's firing, and for years afterward the memory of it still pained me. But when performance issues arise, a leader must act. Rather than dealing with performance issues directly, many move problem employees into positions of little responsibility, setting up a "deadwood" problem from which organizations suffer. Left unattended, the consequences of leaving a problem employee in place often metastasize.

That's why entrepreneurial leaders must become as skilled at firing as they are at hiring. In my career as an operating executive, board member, and investor in hundreds of start-ups, I've had to terminate many people. Indeed, I teach a course at Stanford that focuses on how to have difficult conversations, but some former students joke that most of the class is about firing people.

Like everyone, I still get nervous before I tell people they're being terminated. Nonetheless, I've become adept at this vital and underappreciated task of leadership. People will always need to be let go because it's impossible to be error-free in hiring—to bring on only those who fit with the organization and perform flawlessly. Furthermore, organizations change, roles shift, and even many highly skilled employees can't adapt. People need to move on, and they won't always be the first to recognize it.

What matters as much as actually removing people is *how people are treated* during the process. Every situation is different, and no matter what human resources executives might tell you, there's no way to stick to a standard script when letting someone go. Here are eight ways to be sure you are handling this difficult task as well as possible—and avoid the most common mistakes that leaders make when firing someone.

1. **Don't wait for a "firing offense."** It's natural to procrastinate when deciding to move someone out of a job. Good managers are compassionate and empathetic, and this leads many to repeatedly give underperformers one last chance. Some managers go further, awaiting some dramatic event or ethical breach to clearly justify the firing. Avoid this trap. Building a top team requires constantly assessing the organization and its members—to identify who can grow into larger roles and those whose skills aren't keeping up with new demands. Document the smaller, quieter moments of underperformance and establish a trendline. Try coaching, training, and other methods to fix the problem. But recognize when someone has become what I call a "net drainer"—someone whose performance and attitude have begun infecting the rest of the team. When that situation can't be fixed quickly, it's time to act. Just as when a wide receiver consistently fails to catch the ball, the rest of the team deserves to have a more reliable player on the field.

   In her book *Radical Candor*, Kim Scott, a former faculty member at Apple University and former manager at Google, lists four lies managers tell themselves to avoid firing people: (1) the person's performance will get better; (2) having somebody in the role is better than having nobody while we search to fill it; (3) it's smarter to transfer the person to another department than to fire him or her; and (4) firing the person will be bad for morale. "Most managers wait far too long to [fire people] because they have fooled themselves into believing it's unnecessary," Scott writes.[1]

Don't fool yourself. If someone's performance is eroding and beyond repair, waiting for some dramatic incident to justify dismissal often leads to long delays—and the event you're waiting for could prove more traumatic or costly than you anticipate, both to the person and to the organization.

2. **Be willing to fire friends or family.** One of the reasons organizations have anti-nepotism policies is that once you hire a friend or relative, it can be challenging to fire him or her. Additionally, genuine friendships develop on the job, and these relationships can complicate a manager's duty to make personnel changes. Nonetheless, there can be no sacred cows. Good managers separate friendship from work—and if they bring on a family member (which is common in family-owned firms), they must clearly communicate that this status won't protect the person if he or she underperforms. Too often, companies that coddle managers' friends and family become an employer of last resort for weak talent, because the best employees won't want to stay on such teams.

3. **Don't surprise people.** Subordinates deserve frequent feedback, and this is especially true when someone is underperforming. No one should be surprised when he's fired—and if he is, it's a sign that you've failed not in the termination conversation but in your feedback and evaluation processes. Most firings are not because of a single event; therefore, they should come at the end of several discussions and perhaps after implementing a performance improvement plan (PIP) in which an employee is put on notice (and the problem is clearly

documented). In many cases, putting an employee on a PIP signals the employee to begin looking for work on his own; if his job search is successful quickly, it becomes unnecessary to fire him. This outcome has a number of virtues, including saving money and eliminating litigation risk.

One note about that last point. Fear of being sued by a fired employee drives many of the so-called best practices that HR people advise using when someone needs to be let go. In many cases, this fear is overblown. Unless it involves discrimination or harassment, it's very difficult for a fired employee to successfully sue a former employer—and even if he or she tries, it typically takes years. In medicine, there's research showing that if doctors deal with patients candidly (by, for example, apologizing if they make a mistake), the chances of a malpractice suit drop. The same is true in corporate life. If you give people frequent, honest assessments of their performance, behave fairly and humanely, and don't take them by surprise when you ask them to leave, the odds of a suit are lower than you may fear.

4. **Deliver the message clearly and immediately.** A manager who has decided to let someone go should schedule a meeting and deliver the termination message within the first thirty seconds of sitting down: "We've decided to make a change, to terminate your position, to replace you." To drag it out—which many managers do because of the discomfort they feel delivering painful news—invites misunderstanding and awkwardness. It also gets in the way of moving immediately to next steps—organizing the employee's departure in a way that is most helpful to her and least disruptive to the organization. Throughout the discussion, play it straight: any attempts at humor, or showing sympathy, or at blaming the decision on someone else merely create risk for offense or misunderstanding. The sooner you deliver the basic message and shift the discussion to severance, benefits, and the transition plan, the better.

5. **Don't overexplain the decision.** A termination meeting is a
    time to communicate a decision—not to debate it, defend it,
    or negotiate it. It's natural for people being fired to seek more
    information, to repeatedly ask variations of the question why.
    You needn't offer an elaborate answer; instead, give a simple
    explanation for the performance issues that led to the decision.
    If you've provided feedback and coaching before this conver-
    sation (see "Don't surprise people," above), the terminated
    employee already has sufficient information for why he or she
    will be leaving. Regardless, this meeting isn't about rationale,
    it's about logistics. Specifically, your tasks are to (1) deliver the
    message that they've been terminated and (2) talk through the
    next steps, which include announcing the decision internally
    and externally, and severance arrangements.

    If the person insists on defending himself, your job is to
    sit back and listen, limiting your reactions or responses. Avoid
    the temptation to engage or defend yourself. It's natural for
    someone receiving this news to be emotional, and sometimes
    (depending on your prior relationship and the context) it may
    be useful to have a follow-up conversation with the person
    once emotions recede. In those situations, offer to set up a time
    and place outside the office to meet and talk about the coming
    job search, potential target companies, people in your network
    who might help, what you'll say during a reference check—and
    perhaps your advice on how he or she might be successful in
    their next position. But be aware that in many firings, such
    a follow-up meeting may prove unrealistic. Humans tend to
    develop negative feelings about people who communicate bad
    news, and even if you handle a termination with consideration
    and kindness, your subsequent relationship with this person
    may be difficult.

6. **Be generous.** In the long-term, it is cheaper and generally
    better for the organization—and, of course, for the person

leaving—if the company pays a generous severance package. You are buying peace (because someone who accepts a severance package waives the right to litigate), assuaging some of the guilt you may feel, and giving the terminated employee a fair chance to start over. The package should contain:

- financial severance,
- professional outplacement assistance,
- specific information about compensation for vacation pay and other earned benefits,
- specific information on continuing health insurance,
- a plan for providing references during the job hunt,
- an agreed-upon internal and external communication plan, and
- the signing of a legal release.

The virtues of being generous include saving on legal fees, avoiding potential litigation, and reducing the internal strife, as any employees upset about the firing will hear about the generous terms. In general, severance packages are sized with an eye toward the employee's tenure, but as you make this judgment, recognize that if a new employee has failed to perform, some of the blame falls on the hiring manager for erring, increasing the organization's culpability. It may be counterintuitive, but that should make the company more willing to cover some of the employee's financial losses.

7. **Be human.** Good bosses aren't robots or automatons. They have feelings, and they recognize that employees who are being fired will feel a complex and unpleasant mix of emotions. Managers must deal with them appropriately, which mostly involves listening patiently and avoiding responding with negative emotion of their own. Managers also must realize that though the formal employment relationship is ending, the departing employee likely has many personal relationships with coworkers. Dealing with a fired employee

graciously is about more than manners and courtesy, it's also a business imperative. Industries are small, so the person you're firing today may work for a customer or supplier tomorrow.

8. **Don't hand off the dirty work.** No one likes to fire people. No one likes *being* fired either. (I know this firsthand: it's happened to me.) The only thing people like less than being fired by their boss is to be fired by a hired gun or an HR director. (Remember the Anna Kendrick character in the movie *Up in the Air*?) Many companies hand responsibility for firing to HR executives or professional outplacement people. To me, this is a cold, harsh, and uncaring practice. I've never done it, and I never will.

That's not to say you can't have an HR person involved. It's smart and advisable to rehearse a termination conversation with an HR professional beforehand; he or she has more expertise and experience in this task than most managers, and rehearsing may be the single best way to prepare for difficult conversations. In certain cases, it's useful to have an HR person accompany the manager to the meeting to serve as a witness. An HR person also has the ability to answer technical questions about severance or benefits continuation about which the manager may lack knowledge. My preference is to begin termination conversations one-on-one; this allows the departing employee to save face and not have the decision communicated in front of a third party. After I've done the hard part, I ask HR to join us to talk about the details of the severance arrangement.

There's another common mistake people make when firing a colleague: I call it the "devil made me do it" approach. In this scenario, the manager blames the decision on someone else—the board or some higher-level executive—and seeks to avoid becoming a target of the terminated employee's anger by suggesting "I'm just the messenger." This is a cop-out. The person communicating the decision should take personal responsibility for it—and not pass the buck to others.

Not doing your own firing is a failure to clean up after yourself. Eventually, the whole organization will pick up on your inability to face tough issues. You needn't learn to enjoy doing it—only sadists do. You needn't even come to the point that it doesn't cause anxiety. You simply must get to the point that you do it, the way you do any other unpleasant task. It is a critical part of the job of being an entrepreneurial leader.

Before I begin the conversation to end someone's employment, I engage in a series of self-talk exercises, to put myself in the right mind-set for this difficult conversation. Some of my self-talk emphasizes the need to act with grace and dignity. (*Letting this person go is one of my most important tasks. I will do it with the utmost sensitivity.*) I recall that as a manager, I deserve some of the blame for the failure. (*This results from my mistakes, as well as theirs.*) To avoid becoming defensive, I focus on the end result we both desire. (*I want to help this person find a place where she can maximize her potential—a place that better fits her skills, personality, and ambitions, her style of working.*)

I also focus on my duty to the team to remove an underperformer. This may not be obvious to new managers, but it's something experienced bosses learn over time. Andrew Hoffman learned this lesson early on. At age twenty-four, after graduating with an engineering degree from MIT, Hoffman moved to Nantucket, where he spent five years as a carpenter. Very quickly, he began supervising crews building large custom homes. As a young manager, he frequently had to fire coworkers for chronic lateness, on-the-job drunkenness, or simply being subpar carpenters. During one twelve-month period, he fired fifteen people. He wrote about this experience in his memoir, *Builder's Apprentice*.[2]

Today Hoffman is a professor of management at the University of Michigan, where he teaches students to avoid using euphemisms such as *downsizing* or *rightsizing* or *letting someone go*. "These terms are bloodless and fail to capture the true intensity and anguish that goes with looking someone in the eyes and telling him he's out of a job," Hoffman writes.[3]

Hoffman describes an epiphany that took place while out for a beer with a senior carpenter one evening after firing yet another underperformer. Hoffman was despondent. The older, wiser craftsman told him: "Stop thinking about the guys you fired and start thinking about the guys you still employ. They're the ones who deserve your attention," he said.[4] Graham Weaver, a colleague with whom I teach, describes this as "watering your flowers and cutting your weeds."

Over time, Hoffman recognized that wisdom. "I learned that everyone [on the crew] knew when a person had to go and they were waiting for me to do it," he writes. "And by letting the person go, the people I left behind felt better about working for me. . . . They worked harder, with more pride, as long as I held the whole crew to the same high standard and did my job by weeding out those who didn't meet it."[5]

Like most important skills of management, it's difficult to learn how to fire in the classroom or from a book. It's a skill that's gained through preparation (including role-playing the conversation) and repeated practice—and as unenjoyable as it will be, it's something every leader must learn to do well.

RECAP

▶ As an entrepreneurial leader, your job is to put the best team on the field at all times. You owe it to those who stay to not burden them with those who should move on.

▶ As with any activity that requires skill, removing people from the team takes practice.

▶ Since removing a teammate is an emotional and difficult passage for all, be gracious, generous, and thoughtful, remembering that you, too, failed to make the situation work.

DELIVER
RESULTS

Trust is enhanced by delivering on promises. Missions are refined as results come in. Teams improve based on success. With the foundations of trust, mission, and team in place, it's time to deliver results. The maps in this final section are not intended as a comprehensive "how-to" manual. Instead, they include the practical tips I share with entrepreneurs I coach, the common pitfalls I warn students to avoid, and the mind-sets and self-talk that can help any entrepreneurial leader deliver superior results. To juggle the competing claims of customers, shareholders, and team members, entrepreneurial leaders need checklists and wisdom. The following maps offer guidance for dealing with ten almost-certain challenges.

MAP 1

HOW TO MAKE DECISIONS

When you want something, all the universe conspires in helping you to achieve it.
—Paulo Coelho, *The Alchemist* (1988)

I n 2003, the board of JetBlue faced a very difficult choice.

Since its inception, the airline had modeled itself after Southwest, the low-cost pioneer. One of the ways Southwest keeps its fares low is by flying just one type of aircraft, the Boeing 737. This standardized approach allows it to train pilots and maintenance workers on only the 737, providing a big cost savings. When we launched JetBlue, we'd chosen to use a different aircraft, the Airbus A320, but we mimicked Southwest's strategy and flew a single type of plane.

As JetBlue grew, however, we saw an opportunity to utilize a smaller aircraft to begin flying into a new set of airports. The board had a long series of discussions about whether to invest in a second type of equipment—and if so, which one.

David Neeleman, our founder, was advocating that we become the first airline to fly Embraer's new 190 aircraft. It seats about one hundred passengers in two-by-two seating, offering great passenger space and good legroom. And because the passenger count is lower than other aircraft, it requires fewer flight attendants to service each trip.

As the board weighed the pros and cons, I was quick to back Neeleman's analysis and embrace his desire to become the Embraer 190's "launch customer." After months of debate, the board agreed to the plan. JetBlue placed its order, and in November of 2005, we began flying our first Embraer 190s between Boston and New York.

Looking back, many observers have second-guessed that call and with some reason. The Embraer 190 has been difficult and costly to maintain. On average, our Embraers spend just ten hours a day in the air, compared with almost thirteen hours for our Airbus planes. As Neeleman points out, JetBlue subsequently struck a deal to pay JetBlue's Embraer pilots nearly as much as pilots flying the much more complex A320s; looking back, Neeleman says if he'd known the company would opt for near parity in the pay levels, he never would have advocated for buying the Embraer. In 2018, we placed an order for sixty new Airbus A220s. Many saw that decision as an admission that we made the wrong call back in 2003.

I may be alone in seeing it a bit differently. Choosing to go with the Embraer was not a *perfect* choice, and in the future I would not advocate being a launch customer for any new aircraft, regardless of manufacturer.

However, judged through the lens of revenue and strategy, I look back David's advocacy for JetBlue to begin flying the Embraer as more right than wrong. Without the smaller airplane, we wouldn't have been able to address the secondary markets that became a vital part of JetBlue's growth strategy. If we'd delayed, we might have lost ground (and market share) to rivals. Yes, the plane's costs were higher than we expected, but the new revenue we gained more than offset it; despite the costs, flying those Embraer 190s remained profitable.

When I wrote that going with the Embraer was "not a *perfect* choice," I chose those words intentionally. Entrepreneurial leaders rarely have the luxury of making perfect choices. Instead, they're choosing between imperfect options, making bets in the face of uncertainties, or making a call they know is suboptimal because of constraints that observers or the public may not even recognize.

Decisions are destiny. Making tough ones is the measure of the entrepreneurial leader. If you're making a lot of easy calls, you've failed to delegate. Most of the decisions you make personally should be close calls.

Good decisions are necessary to great execution. Yet some leaders delay making them. Others make them before having the information that would alter the probability of success. Entrepreneurial leaders know big from small, likely from unlikely, and urgent from optional. They tend to know when to take a decision—especially one of the close-vote, 51-percent-to-49-percent variety.

I recall learning in a long-ago psychology class about subjects shooting wadded-up paper balls into a wastebasket. Those with the lowest aptitude for being good decision makers either stood right over the basket so they couldn't miss, or clear across the room, where they couldn't be expected to make the shot. Those with the best wiring for decision making stood at a reasonable but challenging distance, where success depended on a combination of skill, pattern recognition, and good fortune. As I've gained experience, I've observed this ability to learn quickly as being a differentiating factor among the most effective entrepreneurial leaders with whom I've worked.

Since the quintessential job of leadership is to make changes that improve things, entrepreneurial leaders must learn the maps and mind-sets for good decision making.

When leaders are just starting out, their natural decision making equipment tends to be inconsistent. Not only is it untested and unschooled, but it's also been influenced by factors over which they have limited or no control—parents, geography, nationality, health, religion, family resources, and genetic makeup. Leaders may tweak some of these factors over time, but they represent starting points that many accept as destiny.

Fortunately, experience helps fine-tune one's decision making apparatus. Building one small choice upon another, and learning from both wins and losses, I found I could slowly develop wisdom—refining a nascent ability to *predict outcomes*. With this, I found I could have a bigger influence than I'd previously thought possible. I eventually saw that decisions could either lead to more options (and a growing confidence and courage) or fewer options (resulting in more doubt, fear, indecision, and a sense of impotence).

In examining the evolution of my own decisions, and in thinking about the mentoring and advice I give other leaders in my roles as board member, investor, or informal mentor, I have developed the following rules for making tough choices.

1. **Eliminate the excuse that life isn't fair.** Get comfortable with making optimal decisions from the array of *possible* options, rather than wishing you lived in an alternate reality. No amount of wishing will change things. Start with where you are and choose from the alternatives before you.

   Early in my career I read a short book by Peter B. Kyne, *The Go-Getter: A Story that Tells You How to Be One*. Published by William Randolph Hearst in 1921, the book tells the story of Bill Peck, a war vet with a limp and half an arm who approaches his first meeting with a potential employer by refusing to take no for an answer. Peck is soon given an assignment to deliver a blue vase to his potential employer. Facing impossible odds, told no at every turn, and running into circumstances that would discourage anyone, Peck reminds himself of a phrase his commanding officer had drummed into him: "It shall be done." And he overcomes every obstacle. It's a timeless tale of perseverance.[1]

   I was so impressed by the story that I read it aloud to my kids—twice, a decade apart, setting up the concept I called the Blue Vase Award for those who went the extra mile to achieve an objective. Two decades later, when one of my sons was COO of a small company battling larger competitors, he had everyone read the book. They found the story energizing, and they embraced its message. "It shall be done" became a company-wide catchphrase.

2. **Make good small decisions.** Use small decisions as a way to practice pattern recognition, to learn what works and what

doesn't. If you find yourself making one disappointing decision after another, get help to figure out what's leading to bad choices. Usually, the chance to win the big points is earned by winning lots of smaller ones. The decisions we make when we still have training wheels on can either limit or expand our options. So accept that most decisions *do*, in fact, matter— even if they're only giving us practice.

3. **Go into decisions *expecting* they'll work out.** Expectations impact outcomes. If you're obsessed by thoughts of failure soon after making a decision, you should rethink your choice. By imagining winning in vivid detail, you can create positive imagery that inspires—even when early returns disappoint. For many years, I've kept with me a quote from William Hutchinson Murray about the power of commitment:

> Until one is committed, there is hesitancy, the chance to draw back, always ineffectiveness. Concerning all acts of initiative (and creation), there is one elementary truth, the ignorance of which kills countless ideas and splendid plans: that the moment one definitely commits oneself, then providence moves too.[2]

4. **Own your bad decisions.** Owning decisions is a mark of maturity. When we're immature, we blame outcomes on others, or on outside factors. In her book *Thinking in Bets*, Annie Duke, a former professional poker player, cites a study by a Stanford professor in which 75 percent of drivers involved in an auto accident blame someone else—including 37 percent of those involved in a single-car accident in which they are the only driver. (Among the amusing accident reports the study quotes: "I collided with a stationary truck coming the other way.")[3]

With maturity, we learn to own our failures and bad decisions. Then we do something to correct the map. There is information in failure that can improve future decision making. The risk, of course, is in *over*learning the lessons of a bad decision. The danger of overcompensating can be worse than the bad outcome.

5. **Don't let biases drive your choices.** Psychologists have built careers studying the mental gymnastics we engage in that can lead us to make the wrong decision—or justify one after the fact. "Many executives today realize how biases can distort reasoning in business," the Nobel laureate Daniel Kahneman has written (in an article with two coauthors).[4] Among the biases that decision scientists warn against are *confirmation bias* (which leads people to ignore evidence that argues against the direction in which they're leaning), *anchoring* (which describes how people tend to factor one piece of information too heavily in decisions), and *loss aversion* (in which people behave too conservatively to avoid the pain of losing something.)

   In addition to these psychological phenomena, social factors can also create biases. For instance, peer pressure is often a driver when young people approach life's most important choices. Thus helping young managers imagine how their decisions will look in five or ten years is one of the best gifts we can give them. Lots of bad decisions are rooted in expediency, in groupthink, or in wanting to please others. If you're going to live with the outcome of a decision, allow others a voice but not a vote. Invite input, discount it, and maintain control of the decision.

6. **Follow your instincts, not your emotions.** One of the benefits of experience and maturity is the development of instincts. As the writer Malcolm Gladwell describes in his book *Blink: The Power of Thinking Without Thinking*: "We live in a world that assumes that the quality of a decision is directly related to the time and effort that went into making it. . . . We believe that we are always better off gathering as much information as possible and taking as much time as possible in deliberation.

We really only trust conscious decision-making. But there are moments, particularly in times of stress, when haste does not make waste, when our snap judgments and first impressions can offer a much better means of making sense of the world . . . [and when] decisions made very quickly can be every bit as good as decisions made cautiously and deliberately."[5]

While learning to trust your instincts, however, be careful to learn to differentiate instincts from emotions. Instincts are quick, subconscious choices or behaviors that often result from experience and practice. Emotions well up from places we don't often understand—chief among them are anger, jealousy, greed, or fear. Examine how you're feeling (and why) before you pull the trigger on a decision.

One emotion deserves special attention when it comes to decision making: fear. Fear can make you freeze up, but in most business situations, it's better to look the circumstances squarely in the face, make a call, and deal with consequences than to leave things in limbo. Sometimes when I'm tempted to make a decision and realize that I'm relying on emotion, I describe the trade-offs to a friend and explain how I'm leaning and why. More often than not, describing my thinking aloud causes me to pause, to get a better handle on the trade-offs, and to own my decision. Get a second or third opinion from skeptics you trust to see your blind spots—the advisors who'll push back and make you defend your assessments. You're probably not the first person to face a given predicament, so seek out someone who has been there before. Mentors have seen a lot of things. Find a good one if you can. If you can't, make a habit of reading how past leaders have made momentous choices.

7. **Don't make important decisions in haste.** Although it's important not to let fear send you into "analysis paralysis," don't veer
   too far in the other direction and make decisions too hastily if
   there's no urgency to doing so. Imagine you're driving toward

an important fork in the road on a foggy evening with the sun going down, visibility limited, and an imperative to get home. In such a case, smart drivers pull over and take a break. Entrepreneurial leaders do the same thing. Often you'll make a better choice by sleeping on it. Your best decisions will come when you see clearly, optimistically, and in the light of day. As an alternative, I've found that when I temporarily leave the issue behind to deal with an unrelated one, even for a few hours, I often find answers to the decision I've set aside.

8. **Accept that most business decisions have at their core (a) cost–benefit assessments and (b) probabilities associated with an array of potential outcomes.** Many of the choices you make in business will involve a spreadsheet of data. When assessing it, recognize two things: (1) cost–benefit analysis typically fails to recognize or properly account for the full range of costs and downsides and (2) forecasts based on probabilities tend to be too optimistic. We tend to want what we want, so we underestimate costs, overestimate benefits, and skew probabilities in favor of outcomes we hope for. Decision science offers sophisticated tools for some of these situations, but apart from Wall Street, they're rarely used in the typical C-suite. (I learned to do Monte Carlo simulations in business school, but I've never done one in forty-five years of decision making.) At the same time, I never make an important decision without setting up the problem as a simulation with an array of potential outcomes— and thinking hard on whether I've included all potential costs and thoughtfully assessed the probabilities.

9. **Run the decision through the execution screen.** Good decisions can become great ones—if you execute them well. So for every option, consider the ease of execution, the likelihood of team support, and the enthusiasm of relevant third parties. If these are lacking, many *apparently* great decisions will fall apart when moving from paper to action. I'd prefer a relatively

good decision with exceptional execution to a brilliant decision that cannot be executed on time or on budget.

10. **If you make a mistake, correct it.** In the example of the decision to be a launch customer with the Embraer 190 or to break ground on an expensive real estate project, this is hard advice to follow. Indeed, it make take a decade or more to fix a suboptimal decision. But most decisions are reversible with acceptable costs. And the cost of indecision is often higher—if harder to evaluate—than most think.

Leading invariably requires making decisions under conditions of uncertainty. And since information costs money and takes time to assemble and analyze, there comes a point when it makes sense to stop those efforts. Many decisions are no better for gathering more information—and worse for the delay. Thus knowing when you have *just enough* information to pull the trigger makes all the difference.

When I think about the execution phase that follows a decision, a particularly important (and even life-altering) type of decision comes to the front of my mind: marriage.

As I write this, I've been married to Diana for forty-seven years. One can never know how a partner will evolve over the years, or what will be the challenges you face—alone and together. (Talk about conditions of uncertainty!) Some of the best advice I received about the decision to marry is that its outcome depends not on the one big decision (when to propose and to whom) but on the millions of smaller decisions that follow every day.

I recall Stephen Covey once telling the story of a colleague who announced he was getting a divorce. When Stephen asked him why, he responded: "I don't love my wife anymore." Stephen replied: "Well then, love her." His point was simple yet profound. The decision to marry is a high-stakes one made under conditions of massive uncertainty. But the choice to love is the daily, granular, follow-on decision that makes that initial choice good or bad.

While this example may seem inappropriate for a business book, I consider it relevant. Too many decision-makers agonize too long trying to make the perfect decision. That kind of agony fails to recognize that a great decision can result from a marginal one that is followed by adjustment, reframing, pruning, and fixing. I tell my students who are agonizing over which job to take (a First-World problem faced by many Stanford MBAs), to perform well in the role, build great relationships, and adjust if necessary—perhaps going into adjacent orbits. Moving in the right general direction is important; the fine-tuning can happen as more information comes in.

Finally, realize there's a hierarchy of decisions that can be ordered by their impact on our lives. Most far-reaching and hard-to-change decisions arrive in the context of: (1) marriage, (2) children, (3) work, (4) friends, and (5) life's ultimate accountability, which will vary from person to person. (For some, it will be accountability to one's progeny; for others, it will be to an affinity group, God, or some higher power.) If we get good at picking the right direction, and assessing the probabilities of various outcomes (which includes factoring in execution risk), we may find events conspiring to lead us to summits and safely back.

RECAP

- ▶ Decisions are destiny, so take them seriously—but not so seriously that they paralyze you. Most can be fixed.

- ▶ When you make a mistake, admit it, apologize, fix it, and move on determined to learn, developing pattern recognition that allows you to make better decisions next time.

- ▶ It's all the little decisions after the big ones that make the difference. Don't ignore the granular. As an entrepreneurial leader, you need to learn to alternate between flying just above the trees and at thirty thousand feet.

MAP 2

HOW TO SELL

There are worse things in life than death. Have you ever spent an evening with an insurance salesman?
—from *Love and Death* (1975),
written and directed by Woody Allen

started my first business when I was eleven years old. My dad staked out a small plot of land behind our two-bedroom house, provided seeds, and lent me his hoe for a season. I dutifully planted tomatoes, cucumbers, carrots, and squash, then irrigated, cultivated, and harvested the bounty. With help from my six-year-old brother, I went up and down the dirt road of our small central Michigan subdivision with our Radio Flyer wagon, offering fresh vegetables to neighbors.

The most striking thing about this young enterprise is how little we had to do to convince people to buy our product. The fact that my brother was a cute little guy may have given us a slight advantage, but the larger reason was that we were selling something people actually wanted: vegetables that we'd picked just hours earlier, grown in local soil, at a ridiculously low price. The lesson I drew from the experience is that it's incredibly easy to sell something when you're meeting a real customer need.

A couple of years later, in middle school, I had a much different kind of sales experience. My school was trying to raise money, and every student was asked to go door to door selling magazine subscriptions. There were suggested per-student quotas, leaderboards, and prizes given for the student who brought in the most money for the school. Like my classmates, I dutifully took my order pad and began knocking on doors. I hated it. My neighbors who wanted to receive magazines at home generally already subscribed, so they had little need to buy more from a roving band of adolescent subscription pushers. (Thanks to the Internet, this is probably even more true today than it was in the 1950s.) Instead of offering something our customers wanted, it felt like we were begging for money or trying to cajole them to engage in a transaction that was mostly for our benefit, not theirs. At first, I put some effort into this enterprise, but once I realized how little natural demand there was for what we were selling, my heart wasn't in it. My name never made it anywhere near the top of the school's leaderboard, and I didn't care. The primary lesson I drew from the experience is that it's incredibly difficult (and often demoralizing) to be asked to persuade someone to buy something that doesn't solve a real problem or fulfill a need.

No business can survive without sales. To find paying customers—the lifeblood of any business—entrepreneurial leaders must first raise capital, hire great teams, build a brand, and cultivate customer loyalty. Each of these is, in its own way, a kind of sale, even if it doesn't involve the literal purchase of the company's product by a customer. Managers who are presiders may oversee well-oiled institutions without ever needing to ask a customer to buy anything. In contrast, entrepreneurial leaders know that both kinds of selling—the kind that involves the literal exchange of a product for cash and the softer version of convincing outsiders to believe in the goals of the business—are vital to anyone who hopes to start, lead, manage, or preside over a growing business.

Sales is about figuring people out. Great salespeople don't push products—they listen. They solve problems. And they do it all by providing solutions that are worth more to customers than they cost. This is not merely the essence of recruiting lifetime customers, it's the only way to build durable relationships with suppliers, shareholders, and employees.

Listening for ways to solve others' problems is a key to sales—as well as to entrepreneurial leadership.

Think of any great entrepreneur, and there's a good chance he or she is a salesperson at heart. Consider Steve Jobs, Lee Iacocca, Mary Kay, Phil Knight, Sam Walton, Martha Stewart, or Tory Burch.

No matter what industry you choose, having an acute sense of the customer will pay off. And believe it or not, sales can be fun. If you believe in the value of what you're selling, you'll realize that you are in the business of making people happier, more productive, or whatever they are solving for. With this mind-set, sales can be fulfilling in the moment and meaningful in the long run. And if you don't believe in the value of what you're selling, go elsewhere. It won't be long before the market figures out your insincerity.

The least popular (but perhaps most useful) advice I give every year to MBA graduates is to pick up sales experience as soon as possible—and the closer to the customer, the better.

Sadly, very few of my students heed this advice. Of every year's crop of MBA graduates, almost half will go into finance or consulting to avoid the hustle—and rejection—that are part of trying to sell something to flesh-and-blood customers. What they don't realize is that twenty years down the road, many of their most successful classmates will have mastered the art of persuasion and gained the ability to identify an actual need. They will have built their careers on the ability to sell goods and services to flesh-and-blood humans.

Why don't MBAs flock to sales jobs? One reason is a fear that they'll be enlisting in an army of commission-dependent, interchangeable cogs in a business machine. Having just spent two years and a small fortune learning about strategy, finance, and organizational behavior, some feel they are beyond enlisting in the business world's front lines. But they're wrong. And so are the schools that offer few (if any) courses on selling. "Universities [view] sales as 'trade-school' stuff and typically [don't] offer sales-related courses," write Frank V. Cespedes and Daniel Weinfurter in the *Harvard Business Review*. "Even when the boom in MBA programs coincided with the rise of marketing as a discipline, sales was treated like a stepchild at best." According to Cespedes and Weinfurter's research, fewer than a hundred of the four thousand US colleges offer a course on sales, even though 50 percent of US college graduates are likely to work in a sales-related function at some point in their professional lives.[1]

If you're smart enough to spend time in a sales position, you will learn how to do three crucial things beyond the actual selling:

Conquer rejection. Cold calling, smiling and dialing, lead generation—whatever you call it, phoning strangers takes perseverance and the ability to get used to hearing no very frequently. As someone who got his start leasing warehouse space, I can attest to the value of overcoming rejection and developing a granular, customer-by-customer connection with the market. Jobs involving lead generation and lead qualification constitute important, often entry-level corners of the sales funnel that may turn off some would-be sales reps—but these can be great roles to help someone learn a market. Embrace them if that's where you get your start.

Identify and solve problems. Buck Rodgers, the legendary former head of sales for IBM, used to say that his favorite call of the day was from an angry customer. He considered it an opportunity to prove to that person why choosing IBM had been a smart move. After-the-sale service jobs (often called account management) are vital to establishing and maintaining lifetime customers and can serve as a tutorial in what works and what doesn't. Getting direct customer feedback will lead to product improvements and will teach you how to respond to customers before you lose them—and it will make you a product expert as well as a salesperson.

Prepare for bigger jobs. As you master the art of sales, you're honing your powers of persuasion, improving your listening abilities, and developing the grittiness that makes salespeople such durable members of the workforce—all of which happen to be valuable leadership skills that can help you rise to the top and better manage your responsibilities once you're there.

A quote from Zig Ziglar applies here: "You can get everything in life you want if you will just help enough other people get what they want."[2] If a job in sales can teach you that, you shouldn't miss the opportunity. And if you're in finance, consulting, or supply-chain management, there's no reason not to borrow this salesman's credo.

In a start-up, a founder or CEO may spend part of his or her time literally selling, particularly if the firm is pursuing big accounts in a business-to-business (B2B) space. More likely, however, the selling a leader does is the holistic sort of selling that refers to persuading and influencing. An entrepreneurial leader who is recruiting a key new employee is selling. So is one who is lining up financing or arranging a vital vendor relationship.

Frequently, one's ability to persuade will depend on relationship skills rather than transactional skills. Therefore a vital part of the selling a leader does every day is cultivating his or her relationships—what most people call their network. Technology in general, and social media in particular, have made people much more adept at managing networks than in the past. Today many people's first connections with others come through social media—and very often these connections are the first step toward a sale.

Developing a network has similarities to the skills of salesmanship. Both require a focus on what you can do for others before reverting to what they can do for you. It is done slowly and intentionally over time, with a focus on building long-term relationships rather than something that will pay off tomorrow.

Trammell Crow, the larger-than-life developer with whom I began my career, used to advise, "The time to give a Christmas ham is in October, not December." What he meant by that was that the best connections can be formed at unexpected times, via an unexpected call or text or handwritten note whose aim is nothing more than to strengthen the connection. Trammell was a master of this skill, and networking and managing relationships outside the firm were key to the Trammell Crow brand and to his success.

Indeed, great entrepreneurial leaders manage *beyond* the enterprise, *beyond* the strict accountabilities of their firm, and *beyond* the immediacy of the next transaction. They follow what some have called "the law of accelerating returns"—the more you share, the more others share in return as the rate of relationship building and the power of the collaborations accelerate.

By doing a stakeholder analysis, the entrepreneurial leader will recognize the broad array of actors who will play a role in the firm's success. They may include suppliers, distributors, manufacturers, creditors, investors, lawyers, accountants, consultants, travel agents, and on and on, who together form the ecosystem that sustains the life of the enterprise. Smart entrepreneurial leaders nurture this ecosystem, giving everyone an emotional stake in its success. Most importantly, they do so when it's unexpected and *before* it's necessary. This involves a subtle form of selling.

Once a business has a viable economic proposition and base of customers, entrepreneurial leaders may be less involved in day-to-day selling. But there is one type of customer to whom he or she will pay special attention: the *unhappy* customer. If something goes wrong and a customer is unhappy, leaders should want to know exactly why. Clearly, there are some customers whose loss would only improve the bottom line and the well-being of the team. This is rare, however. When dealing with unhappy customers, I strive to do two things: (1) Discern whether I'm dealing with a customer with a problem or with a problem customer. (2) When in doubt, assume it's the former, and work to remind the customer why she chose to do business with us in the first place.

Far more often than not, complaints come from customers with a real problem or a legitimate disappointment. And most customers—and virtually every other constituency—will respond to a show of respect, to a recognition of their interests, and to a logical solution—one that coincidentally will build the brand and legacy of the firm in a way that a merely satisfied customer never will. Done well, dealing quickly and generously with a problem can have positive viral implications and create long-term value.

Smart entrepreneurial leaders schedule time every day for relationship building—even if it's just a few minutes at the beginning of the day, at lunchtime, or at the close of business.

In addition to reaching out to customers and subordinates, no other relationship is more important to a leader than one with peers. While many manage up and down (north and south), it is how one manages east and west (working with peers) that often determines outcomes. These interactions, too, are a form of subtle selling, of persuading.

As social animals, humans thrive when they have strong, high-trust, harmonious relationships with others. At work, this means higher productivity and greater creativity, with less time spent on politics. Great entrepreneurial leaders nurture strong interpersonal relationships that are rooted in trust, respect, openness, and kindness.

Selling and networking are uncomfortable for many. In a 2014 study, three business school professors found that people who engaged in networking felt dirty—to the point where they felt the need to sanitize their hands afterward.[3] Selling can generate similar feelings of discomfort. As journalist Daniel Pink observed: "To the smart set, sales is an endeavor that requires little intellectual throw weight—a task for slick glad-handers who skate through life on a shoeshine and a smile. To others it's the province of dodgy characters doing slippery things—a realm where trickery and deceit [win out] . . . the white-collar equivalent of cleaning toilets—necessary, perhaps, but unpleasant and even a bit unclean."[4]

Successful entrepreneurial leaders get over these feelings. They recognize that leading others requires not just managing inside the organization but *managing out*—that is, growing and nurturing a robust network of external contacts and trusted relationships. And they do it with a clean conscience because their interest in meeting needs is genuine.

Managing a network takes work. Think of yourself as a platform that increases in value the more people use it. Don't worry about a return. Think about your network the way tech venture investors think about "eyeballs," usage, and virality before worrying about profits. Serving your network creates demand, which means increasing the supply of whatever you're providing which, in turn, increases demand.

Go through your list of contacts and create categories—family, employees/partners, associates, investors, suppliers, teachers, neighbors—whatever makes sense for the network you're building. Build a spreadsheet that segments people by category. Keep track of your interactions with them so you will know when the last time you spoke, or sent a note, or a gift, or did a favor. Recognize that each person in your network represents another network that can grow yours exponentially. (LinkedIn demonstrates the power of these second- and third-degree contacts.) But take care not to have an ulterior motive. Don't keep score or expect favors to be returned. Stay in touch, with no expectations. Most will yield nothing but vague goodwill, but do favors and give service anyway. And over a lifetime, you'll have an "account" with hundreds, if not thousands, of people upon whom you can call or for whom you may be able to provide assistance.

RECAP

▶ Imagine sales as a way to delight others, to solve their problems, to make their lives better—and become adept at it.

▶ Consider customer service a form of sales. Put as much energy and attention into it as when making initial sales.

▶ Build and nourish a network without regard to instant returns. Imagine planting trees under which a next generation will sit.

MAP 3

HOW TO NEGOTIATE

Like it or not, you are a negotiator.

—Roger Fisher and William Ury,
Getting to Yes (1981)

I n the early 1980s, my colleagues at Trammell Crow Company and I faced an opportunity. Our company already controlled millions of square feet of warehouse space in Los Angeles, which gave us a dominant and profitable position in an important market. The US government had just announced plans to sell off nearly one hundred acres of land that had once comprised the Cheli Air Force Station, and this parcel had the potential to become a valuable addition to our real estate holdings in Los Angeles.

The government was going to sell the land to the highest bidder, and several companies were interested. We had a deal team of experts looking at the issue from several angles: What was the fair market value of the land? What was its profit potential if we acquired it? How much would our other properties be hurt if a competitor bought and developed it? And based on whatever intelligence we could gather, what were competitors likely to bid for it?

After many hours of careful analysis, the team presented its findings. They concluded that since we were the big kahuna in this market, we really *had* to win the bid for the land; to let it go to a competitor would be costly, both strategically and financially. Based on their best guess at what competitors might pay for it, the team presented two numbers. The first represented the bid they felt would give us a 75 percent chance of winning the property. The second represented the bid that they felt with 95 percent confidence would allow us to prevail. As CFO, I was asked for my opinion on what to bid.

I started out with the higher number, and then I nudged it up to increase our chances even further. This was an important deal, so I wanted a cushion.

When the seller opened the bids, we won, but at a steep cost—we'd bid several *million* dollars more than the second-place bid. Many of my colleagues felt heartburn and regret over this outcome. I understood their disappointment, since we'd paid significantly more than we had to for the land. This excessive spending would drive down our potential profits.

Nonetheless, I was thrilled. We'd won. We paid a price we were comfortable with. If we'd bid a few thousand less and lost, we'd have regretted it. Instead of fretting over our excessive bid, we needed to begin the hard work of developing and leasing the space to ensure a high return on investment—which, looking back on it years later, we achieved comfortably.

As this story illustrates, I view negotiations differently from how many people do, and I tend to disregard some of the tactical advice that's commonly found in negotiation handbooks. Negotiations are not zero-sum games, in which one side wins and the other loses. If you look for it, very often there's a way to find a solution in which both parties feel like they've won. Indeed, this is the bargain that ensures future negotiations—one of the outcomes for which I'm often solving.

Negotiations are a specialized form of conversation—one that determines the give-get that allows people to move forward understanding the costs and benefits of their choices. As with selling and networking, negotiating makes many people uncomfortable. In the United States, unless your job involves frequent negotiation, most of what you buy will involve a fixed price; for many people, the only times they negotiate purchases are for houses and automobiles. (And, in the latter category, some dealerships have moved to no-haggle pricing to appeal to consumers who are uncomfortable negotiating.) The best way to get comfortable negotiating is to do it frequently. Working in the real estate industry, as I did for the first decades of my career, is a wonderful venue for this, since every transaction is subject to negotiation. Engage in this process enough times, and you get comfortable with it.

A good starting point for a successful negotiation is figuring out what the other party wants and finding a way to give it to him without jeopardizing your own position. When you realize your job is to set the price for helping your counterparty achieve his or her objectives, you'll begin to develop a successful approach.

Solve for fairness. Ensure respectful discussion. Seek to be respected, not loved. Allow other parties to "win" without meaning that you have to "lose." And above all, don't resort to theatrics, hollow threats, ultimatums, or bluffing.

When most people think of negotiations in a business context, they think of a highly stylized and often adversarial process where opposing parties with conflicting positions come together to argue their claims. They envision a room filled with teams of people—executives, aides, consultants, bankers, attorneys, and others—each defending their positions in a contentious, tension-filled battle of will and skill. In the most extreme cases, these battles play out through formal arbitration or in a courtroom at the hands of trained litigators.

Those outcomes become much more likely when lawyers are involved. Lawyers are trained to be win-lose gladiators. If you hire one, expect negotiations to take longer, to be episodic rather than serial, and, too often, conflict ridden.

Consistent with these adversarial views, many people also think that the primary purpose of business negotiation is to maximize immediate economic gain. In many cases, getting the best financial outcome is equated with beating the opponent, coming out on top, and proving that one party is right while the other is wrong. The outcomes of such negotiations are determined by who has the most power, whether by virtue of caring less, bluffing better, or holding the better cards.

Given the stakes, it's not surprising that an entire industry has sprung up to provide training and advice for people wanting to hone their negotiation skills. These scholars and so-called experts offer rules and techniques aimed at making managers better negotiators and promising to increase the odds that they—and not their opponents—will get the upper hand.

Not to be outdone by the advisors, attorneys stand ready to offer parties protection on the back end, providing assurance that negotiated agreements will be upheld. The attorneys' job is to memorialize the agreements through the creation of elaborate contracts backed by the threat of the tort system. In most cases, these contracts are designed to be so obscure that the average person will need to hire a separate team of lawyers to decipher them.

Because negotiations are viewed as contests with winners and losers, many of the concepts and techniques suggested by the experts are designed to help people outwit (or intimidate) their adversaries and protect their interests. Some of these techniques are useful; many are not. In fact, a lot of them simply miss the boat and fail to understand the larger role that negotiations play in a leader's success.

Entrepreneurial leaders view negotiations quite differently. Negotiations are prevalent not only in our professional lives but also in our day-to-day interactions with family and friends. Negotiations are how people navigate life—at work, at home, and everywhere in between. Rather than taking a narrow, adversarial perspective that focuses solely on economic gain, entrepreneurial leaders see negotiations as more nuanced. They recognize that good negotiating skills are important for more than making good deals. They are critical to building one's brand as a leader and forming a network of durable long-term relationships. Negotiations are a preamble to opportunity.

As with litigation, negotiations can be stressful and sometimes over-whelming. They generally elicit strong feelings including anxiety. While intellectually you may know all the correct principles and techniques, it can be difficult to stay grounded and make the right calls in the heat of the moment. Having the right mind-sets can make a difference. To the extent you internalize such self-talk, it may guide your approach as well as your demeanor, improving your odds of success as skilled negotiator:

1. **This is but one conversation in a longer narrative.** Over the course of your career you'll engage in thousands of negotiations. Earning a reputation for getting your way at any cost is not what you want to be known for. I've seen this mistake frequently. At Trammell Crow Company, we hired many promising young people who were often promoted into partner roles by their late twenties or early thirties. These jobs required frequent negotiation, and too many of these inexperienced negotiators pursued win-lose deals. "There was this phrase that was often used during that era at Trammell Crow," recalls my former colleague Bob Sulentic. "It was 'I carved him up.'" As the firm's leader, I emphasized that carving someone up is not the goal, reminding everyone that the person you "carve up" today is probably going to sit across from you again in the future. "Relationships come back around. We all know that in our forties, fifties, or sixties, but you haven't personally experienced that when you're twenty-eight or twenty-nine," Bob says.[1] The sooner people learn it, the better.

2. **Consider the other side's interests.** Conceding that your counterparty's interests are legitimate conveys respect and empathy. If they can see you've made an effort to understand their perspective, they're likely to be less defensive and more willing to engage in honest dialogue, making it easier to find a solution that everyone sees as a win. Think of your goal as putting a fair price on what the other party wants. It's up to them to decide if their demands are worth the price you've set. You'll know you're getting close when (1) you can describe their needs in a way that satisfies them, and (2) they can acknowledge the price of what they're asking for.

3. **Directness beats psych-out tactics.** Many people start negotiations by assessing who has more legal or economic firepower, and who's more willing to walk away. Some try psychological techniques to enhance this power status; they might include using personal insults to undermine you, or having two negotiators who utilize the classic good-cop/bad-cop routine.[2] This power-only mind-set may get a deal done; however, it can also go wrong by getting things off on the wrong foot. You might try to avoid this by first focusing on principles both sides agree on.

4. **Aim to create value for all parties.** This flies in the face of Hollywood's last-man-standing version of negotiation. But if your "opponent" benefits from doing business with you, and you walk away satisfied, too, you've created two wins instead of one. Strengthening your relationship with the other party can mean more business, more referrals, a stronger brand, and more durable agreements.

5. **There's power in inquiry.** Most people will tell you what they want out of the negotiations if you ask the right questions. Professional negotiators call this having an *investigatory mind-set*. In negotiation, as in life, doing more listening than talking is a good rule of thumb—and the best negotiators are adept at asking questions. In commercial transactions, you'll usually be negotiating five primary issues: (1) price, (2) terms, (3) time frames, (4) representations and warranties, and (5) remedies. Asking probing questions about the other party's perspective on each of these can yield insights into how to structure the deal. If the other side tells you their chief concern is price, for example, you may be able to set the other terms if you're willing to meet their price number. Understanding the interdependence of these five elements can help make for win-win agreements.

6. **Keep emotions in check.** When negotiations are governed by facts and principles—rather than posturing and tactics—there

is no reason to become emotional during the discussion. Understanding the other party's interests, constraints, and personal situation can help you put things in perspective and keep emotions in check. Still, because negotiations often spark feelings of anxiety or even anger, it can pay to be attentive to your own and your counterparties' emotions during negotiations—and to manage them. When other parties become emotional, step away or attempt to cool things off. Don't react to provocation. Learn to ignore some things. Be especially wary of two situations. First, if the emotions expressed during a negotiation make you feel uncomfortable, resist the urge to concede or wrap up the negotiation too quickly, just to get away from the unpleasant feelings. Second, be especially wary if you or the other party begin to feel angry, since that emotion increases the odds of the negotiation becoming deadlocked. As Harvard Business School professor Alison Wood Brooks writes, "Bringing anger to a negotiation is like throwing a bomb into the process, and it's apt to have a profound effect on the outcome."[3]

7. **Choose counterparties wisely.** Finally, keep in mind that you want to choose the people you're negotiating with whenever you can. It's tough to hold productive discussions with people who get no joy out of the process, and who prefer bare-knuckle fighting over finding creative solutions to challenging problems. As Trammell Crow used to remind me, "You can't do good business with bad people." Similarly, you can't come to fair and lasting agreements with people whose only concern is their own short-term gain. Remember the old saying, "Never wrestle with a pig; you both get dirty and the pig likes it." While you can't always choose with whom you'll negotiate, over a lifetime of brand building as a fair negotiator, you'll more likely find your market.

In Hollywood's stylized version of business negotiations, executives fight a verbal battle from either side of a conference table. Traps are laid, power asserted, and threats made until one side maneuvers the other into a corner. Up steps the Gordon Gekko character to coldly declare himself the victor: "It's not a question of enough, pal. It's a zero-sum game—somebody wins, somebody loses."[4]

But entrepreneurial leaders negotiate with the big picture in mind. How you treat counterparties during a negotiation affects not only the outcomes of the immediate transaction but, more importantly, your reputation and future opportunities—in short, your personal brand. As Roger Fisher and William Ury point out in their classic guide *Getting to Yes: Negotiating Agreement Without Giving In*, your goal is to bring your negotiating partners to their senses, not to their knees.

RECAP

▶ Think of negotiation as a conversation—one in which you're "solving for fair." Imagine negotiations as serial, not episodic, and use them to build a brand: a reputation that will follow you for your entire career.

▶ Extracting one killer deal can turn out to be costly in the long run, because you may forfeit a chance to do more business with a counterparty or simply have to live with an unstable agreement.

▶ Treating a negotiation as a boxing match will mean a lot of unnecessary headaches—and punches that should have never been thrown.

MAP 4

HOW TO RAISE CAPITAL

We spent a lot of time talking about markets and technology, and we have a lot of opinions . . . but the decision should be around people.

—Mark Andreessen

Wrapping up year-end grades, I heard a knock at the door. It was Andy Dunn, a student I hadn't seen in the previous eighteen months. While Andy had been studying for his MBA at Stanford, he'd created a business plan to import a type of South African beef jerky (called biltong) to the United States. I know a bit about the snack-food business, where success requires outfoxing dominant competitors like PepsiCo, and I was frank with him: this was a *really* bad idea. When he came back to meet with me, I worried he hadn't let the beef jerky idea go yet.

Luckily, he hadn't come to see me about biltong. Instead, he told me about Bonobos, the men's pants start-up he and his classmate Brian Spaly were launching. I invited him to practice his pitch to me, and I listened politely, if skeptically.

The more I listened, the more he reminded me of David Neeleman when launching JetBlue. Like David, Andy hoped to disrupt incumbents in a well-established industry. Instead of flying planes, Andy would revolutionize how men bought pants. Andy had an obvious passion for delighting customers and for making a difference in their lives—one of the traits I look for in entrepreneurs. Andy also showed flexibility and a willingness to tweak his plans as he received more customer feedback. But still . . . pants over the Internet?

To my *own* surprise, I wrapped up the meeting by informing Andy—after just forty minutes of presentation—that I'd be his first investor. I offered $100,000—hardly enough to do what he needed but enough maybe to attract others. Soon, a well-known venture capital investor matched my investment, giving Andy and Brian additional credibility, and they were off to the races.

Along with a check, I gave the duo advice. "Money has faces," I said, making clear I was not referring to Alexander Hamilton, Andrew Jackson, or Benjamin Franklin. "Who sits around the table with you at inception can make or break you, so when you pitch investors, know that you're interviewing them as much as they're interviewing you. Think about mutually solving for fit, instead of simply making a pitch. Early on, you want financial partners who'll bring more than just money."

A year later, Andy and Brian had run through their initial seed capital and began seeking a $1 million Series A round. Giddy about their value having tripled in a year, they proposed a new $10 million valuation and asked if I'd come in for the next round at that value. I congratulated them and said I'd double down on my $100,000 investment. When I returned from a trip, however, their valuation had ballooned from $10 million to $15 million—from a 300 percent to 500 percent increase in value in a single year. Troubled by their unilateral valuation increase, I was worried that they might be putting themselves on an impossible trajectory that could make raising future rounds—when it *really* mattered—more challenging, even enterprise threatening. With the sudden explosion of value, I reported I wasn't sure, after all, that I'd invest more money.

Andy emailed me. "We acknowledge that we have some egg on our face with this one," he wrote. "The reality is the round got dramatically oversubscribed at the same time as the business was outperforming our expectations." He talked about this round as an opportunity to "separate the wheat from the chaff" and how "the best deals are always overpriced." He concluded: "Let us know by midweek if you want to participate."[1]

Was I "chaff" to be separated from the wheat they'd suddenly attracted? Were the best deals always overpriced? Were the few percentage points of ownership they were saving for themselves worth running off a founding investor and potential trail guide?

I responded with a long email of my own. I wrote, in part: "I'm left with congratulating you for the success that has brought you to such conclusions, and I sincerely hope it continues." I told him I wouldn't be investing in the second round at the higher valuation, and I offered to sell him my existing shares back at a 20 percent discount—a $12 million valuation. "This will enable you to facilitate a bargain offer to your other early-stage investors, winnow out the 'chaff,' and leave you with a clean slate to move forward with the right investors," I said. My tone made clear I wasn't happy with the way Andy and Brian had changed their terms and communicated their decision to me.

Years later, Andy has talked with me and many others about how much he regrets the way he handled this situation—and what he wishes he'd done differently. To summarize the advice he's given as a guest in my classes:

1. Disagree in person. Spoken words die, but emails live forever. Email is ultimately a cowardly medium for conflict.
2. In a disagreement, you forfeit the right to the "why" of the argument if you screw up the "how" of your approach in disagreeing.
3. Always be willing to revise your position. The ability to retreat from a position is as valuable as the ability to form one.
4. Your founding investors are like the "parents" of your venture. Always honor them as such.

Without my ever saying a word, he'd learned what I consider lifelong lessons for dealing with founding capital providers. While I skipped Bonobos's A round, I invested in following rounds, and I even joined the board, where I served for years as a sort of lead director.

The most important takeaway for entrepreneurial leaders from this awkward incident: When dealing with founding investors and others providing early funding, see them as customers. Their capital is uniquely valuable, but so are the credibility, advice, and relationships they may offer you.

Successful entrepreneurial leaders don't need to be financial wizards, but they do have to know the basics—and they have to get them right. To me, the basics revolve around three simple questions: who are the right investors, how much capital should we raise, and what process is most effective?

Figuring out how much capital to raise for a particular business plan depends on a number of factors: rate of growth, cost of capital investment required, and the cost of product development and marketing. It's unique to each business. Helping you come up with a number is beyond the scope of this book, so talk to advisors, bankers, and other mentors for assistance.

Another question to think about is how much of the financing should come from debt and how much from equity. One of the few cases I recall from my courses at Harvard Business School involved a New England boat builder. During the discussion in class, students tore mercilessly into his overreliance on debt—especially when they heard he'd been forced to hide under his desk from creditors. Near the end of the discussion, the professor identified an incognito visitor in the back of the room: it was the hapless entrepreneur, who came to the front of the class to defend his actions. As I listened to him, all I could think of was never to take on *any* debt. The irony, of course, is that I promptly went to work for a real estate developer, in an industry where heavy leverage is *de rigueur*. Suddenly, debt was the highway to riches. Eventually, I figured out where leverage was my friend and where it risked becoming my jailer.

The question of how much financing to line up can determine whether a business survives. Many businesses fail that might have succeeded with a little more time and/or a less debt. Successful entrepreneurial leaders learn where that line is—perhaps by relying on advice from older, wiser mentors. Where one draws the line depends on whether revenue is recurring, what level of customer loyalty one can count on, how much product stickiness one enjoys, how much costs might vary, what competitors are up to, and, of course, the debt rate, covenants, and repayment schedule. When analyzing these factors, focus on the fundamental economic equation for a successful business—to consistently make a return on capital that exceeds the overall cost of capital (debt plus equity). Anything else is a slow-motion dance that will lead to insolvency.

Sometimes a leader's sense of how much capital is necessary changes dramatically as the business scales. When David Neeleman launched JetBlue, he raised $135 million of equity capital, the most of any airline launch to that point. After a period of growth, we needed *another* $300 million to survive a several-billion-dollar mountain of debt. Today, some would say that JetBlue has one of the best balance sheets in the industry—not the biggest, but the one with the most capacity to survive downturns and to take advantage of size-appropriate market opportunities. That's the flexibility that equity capital (if available) gives a growing venture.

The problem, of course, is that equity capital is expensive. Taking too much equity can make management teams risk-averse or wishing they still owned the more significant economic stake they traded away for security. On the other hand, too much debt puts everything at risk and often mandates short-term fixes that reduce long-term options. To make matters worse, the "Goldilocks zone" (meaning the *just right* amount of leverage) is different for each industry, for each management team, and for each cycle.

I've spent most of my career in real estate and airlines, two extremely capital-intensive businesses that tend to operate with lots of debt financing. Airlines use debt to finance expensive planes, which also generate depreciation to shelter profits, increasing free cash flow. But the airline business is fundamentally different from real estate, in two important ways: (1) aircraft depreciation is real, meaning planes get old and lose value, whereas buildings tend to appreciate in value over time; and (2) airlines have to sell tickets to monetize their airplanes every day, whereas building owners have predictable three- to twenty-five-year leases and a more stable, contractual cash flow. All of this suggests that any sentient leader leverages an airline at lower levels than a real estate ownership company.

Bottom line: wise entrepreneurial leaders constantly watch the weighted average cost of capital and keep an eye out for any deterioration of margin.

Beyond thinking about the kinds of early investors he or she wants, and how much equity and debt should be used, successful entrepreneurial leaders consider these recommendations when they think about the process of raising capital and financing operations and growth:

1. **Hire a pro to review/scrub your plan.** An experienced CFO can refine your projections and add credibility to your efforts to raise capital.

2. **Make your business plan easy to read.** Recognize that some lenders, venture capitalists, angels, and private equity sources have to look at thousands of plans a month.

3. **Lead with a one- to two-page executive summary.** This is the most important section, since it's all many recipients will read. Also include a customer/prospect list (to show evidence of momentum); updated financial statements and projections (be clear on assumptions—some numbers will always be wrong); and a list of the current management team (include bios for any new members). Scrub your report for phrases that signal red flags to sophisticated investors, including "there's no competition for what we do," "the untapped market is enormous," or "our projections are hyperconservative."

4. **Consider the pros/cons of using an agent.** Some brokers and/or investment banks can be very helpful in providing access to potential investors and credibility you'd not otherwise have. Professional guidance can help you wind up with a stronger, more credible group of founding investors—possibly at better terms.

5. **Start with personal relationships first and warm introductions second.** Your time is valuable, and people who know you are more likely to turn into investors.

6. **If turned down, ask for a two-minute favor.** Ask the investor to explain the rejection—not to try to change anyone's mind but to learn how to improve.

7. **Consider market timing.** Don't be afraid of raising capital in a downturn. There's less "noise." It's easier to recruit and retain people. You can find space you can afford, and used equipment and furniture is far less expensive than new. Plus, in a soft market the compelling entrepreneurial leader can get meetings with investors and can be methodical in building a solid culture for when the market returns. According to research by the Kauffman Foundation, half of the companies in the Fortune 500 were launched during a recession or bear market, including General Electric, General Motors, IBM, Microsoft, and CNN.[2]

8. **Plan on being partners for a long time.** Be gracious. Thank people for their time and attention. Remember that over a long career, you're likely to meet capital providers again and again, either by reputation or in person. You're recruiting friends and supporters as much as you're looking for capital.

One final thought about choosing and dealing wisely with early sources of capital: more than in the past, you should be prepared to maintain these relationships for quite some time. During the 1990s in particular, start-ups often went public just a few years after their founding, returning their original capital (often with healthy returns) to their VCs and early investors and then commencing life in the public markets. When choosing a VC in this atmosphere, the relationship between founder and early investor might be remarkably short lived.

This is no longer the norm. Today companies are waiting longer before going public, due to the abundance of private capital, the new complexities required of public companies (due to Sarbanes-Oxley and other regulations), and new methods to let founders and early employees cash in some of their shares without a public offering.

In this environment, a founder may be dealing with early investors for a decade or more—which makes it even more important to select them for certain attributes and to nurture these relationships with special care.

RECAP

► Interview potential sources of capital the way you would a new recruit. They bring more than just capital. The best bring ideas, contacts, and support. The worst bring headaches.

► Too much debt can imperil the business. Too much equity can make it hard to earn a return that exceeds your weighted average cost of capital. Pay close attention to capital structure, because it can influence success or failure.

► Raise capital before you need it. Waiting too long can reduce options, making it harder to get the resources you need.

MAP 5

HOW TO COMMUNICATE

Words are sacred. They deserve respect. If you get the right ones, in the right order, you can nudge the world a little.
—From the play *The Real Thing* (1982),
written by Tom Stoppard

A t JetBlue, a member of our executive crew sends out a weekly email to all twenty-five thousand crewmembers to make sure they never learn news about the airline from the press. At Trammell Crow Company, I sent out a biweekly letter to all partners to keep everyone informed. And at Peterson Partners, I regularly write for the websites of LinkedIn, Forbes, CNBC, and Fortune to share with people inside and outside our organization the principles I think good leaders (including those running our portfolio companies) should consider when managing for success. Heck, I even write a weekly email to my children to let them know what's going on in my and Diana's life.

Leaders communicate all the time, whether they intend to or not, if only because others are watching them. While they may think employees communicate back transparently, the truth is that most people in most organizations don't tell leaders what they think. Similarly, people in most organizations don't understand leaders' priorities, and they rarely think they're getting enough information.

Things are even worse once you go outside the organization. The media—print and electronic—often get things wrong. In most cases they don't do it intentionally, but they can't know details of rapidly developing stories the way industry insiders do. This can lure leaders into either fighting with the media or ignoring them. That's usually a mistake. A well-known adage about the media goes something like "Never pick a fight with someone who buys ink by the barrel and paper by the ton." While still true today, now one must also worry about those with lots of Twitter followers, search engine optimization (SEO) expertise, or massive bandwidth.

While there are well-established techniques for dealing with all matters of communication, a key starting point is to assume that people pick up on nuance. If things aren't going well, say so. But don't stop there. Say what you plan to do to fix them. Don't pull punches. Rarely will you get in trouble for bringing people into the tent too early. If shown the respect of confidantes, many will rise to the challenges you've shared with them.

There are three ways leaders typically fall short in their communication efforts. The first is quantity. Most simply don't communicate enough. Consumed by strategizing, problem solving, and decision making, they forget to inform others of plans, decisions, and progress. They assume information is flowing through the organization and that people are getting what they need from direct supervisors. Unfortunately, communication gaps widen from level to level until—just as in the telephone game kids play as an ice breaker—the cumulative error is exposed, the same way rumor and gossip spread false information in the larger world. If your message can be misinterpreted, it will be.

The second mistake is thinking one can control the message by making communications one way. Authentic dialogue requires giving up control—listening as well as speaking. Well-planned exchanges in controlled settings, with formal presentations by leaders who define the topic and the underlying assumptions, are better than silence. They allow a leader to impart a specific message, control the discussion, and limit diversions. But that's about it. The problem with controlling the discussion is that people mistrust both the messenger and the message. The communication is one way and its (limited) success is measured by whether the message came across as leaders intended, not whether it has recruited commitment or enthusiasm.

The third way leaders undershoot the potential of communication is by failing to communicate directly and honestly. Jack Welch argues that a lack of candor is "the biggest dirty little secret in business."[1] By lack of candor he's not talking about blatant dishonesty (though this does occur). He's talking about a lack of frankness, of sugarcoating bad news and staying quiet rather than presenting people with unpleasant information. In this, constructive criticism is rare, and ideas that could stimulate real debate or challenge the status quo rarely surface.

Those who would like to act as entrepreneurial leaders will need to look at communication differently. For them, communication is about more than relaying information. It's about creating engagement, surfacing ideas, generating trust, and building commitment. Entrepreneurial leaders understand that managers who manipulate and spin won't be seen as open, truthful, and trustworthy.[2]

Entrepreneurial leaders don't want distance and distortion; they want connection. They neither pretend to have all the answers, nor do they deny having preferences. They strive to remain open to influence. Entrepreneurial leaders—like most presider-leaders—communicate with a message and an agenda. The difference is that they *interact* with people. They listen at least as much as they talk. And they learn from other perspectives and experience.

In short, entrepreneurial leaders communicate from a mind-set of participation, not control. They believe that two-way candor builds trust. And they understand that when they spin messages and manipulate communication, they destroy trust, stifle interaction, and erode the very foundation of an innovative, vibrant organization in which everyone has ownership of its future.

Leaders learn the skills of communicating through training and practice. As anyone who has witnessed a gifted off-the-cuff orator can attest, life is not fair, and some people simply are born better at this part of life than others. But most people can get there with focused, intentional hard work.

Beyond seeking out training and engaging in real practice to try to get better, the entrepreneurial leader can also improve by adopting the right mind-set—a disposition and an intention to use the spoken word to create a high-trust, high-engagement environment in which everyone feels it is safe to be candid and forthright. Here are five specific mind-sets I believe will help any leader communicate more openly and more successfully:

1. I HAVE VALID VIEWPOINTS AND CAN MAKE A VALUABLE CONTRIBUTION.

The first step in communicating effectively is knowing you have something important to say. A very capable Stanford PhD told me that she goes into meetings with the same silent reminder: *My perspective is valuable. It's not the only perspective, and it may not be the full story. But I have information that others lack that could be helpful to them. By sharing directly and honestly, I may be able to help others improve their performance and achieve their goals.* These obvious truths were, for her, an important starting point. They reminded me, as leader, that not everyone is confident their ideas will be listened to, and it's my job to lower these barriers.

2. I CAN BE INFLUENCED BY NEW INFORMATION.

Successful communicators remain open to influence. Remember, communication is an interactive process. Like ballroom dancing, you can't do it alone. Great dancers adapt to the movements of their partners so they don't trip and fall on their faces. It's much the same with communication. You have to go in knowing something about the music and the dance steps, but in order to dance well with others (and achieve your objectives) you have to adjust your steps in response to your partner's. You will never be successful if you waltz when the music has changed to a salsa. To remain open and receptive to other views, remind yourself that other people—your colleagues, team, customers—have valuable information and experience. They may see something you're missing. Remain open to change throughout the process. No one gets it right all the time.

3. I AM GENUINELY CURIOUS.

Genuine curiosity is rarely threatening. In fact, truly desiring to understand another's experience shows respect and opens other to being influenced by you. A few simple scripts can help keep you on track. Tell yourself: *I know my intentions, but I don't know theirs. I know only the impact their actions have had on me (and maybe others). I want to understand what they are thinking and what impact I am having on them. I want to understand what data they are operating from as well as their reasoning. What am I missing? What are they missing? I want to start by focusing on their agenda rather than simply clarifying mine.*

The first goal is to understand—not to show others how smart you are. Seeking to understand changes fundamentally the tone and tenor of interactions.

4. OUR GOAL IS FOR THE BEST IDEA TO WIN.

One of the benefits of listening is that it makes you less susceptible to your own ego. When you have a goal that lies beyond you, you are less likely to worry about making yourself look good. You are also less likely to overcomplicate things and talk in vague generalities designed to blur your intentions and hedge your bets. When people look beyond self-interests, they feel greater commitment to the collective good. They engage and give more of themselves.

Here's the self-talk that keeps me centered on others: *This is not about me, it's about them. It's about helping them to be the best they can be. If I feel angry or upset, it's a function of my own self-esteem, self-image, and self-doubts.*

5. I WILL BALANCE INQUIRY WITH ADVOCACY.

Listening alone rarely produces the action needed for a business to thrive and adapt. After listening, entrepreneurial leaders usually have a viewpoint to express—and they have a duty to share it in a way that supports a mutual exchange of information and ideas, then turns into a decision that can be implemented. Peter Senge and his colleagues refer to this productive communication approach as balancing inquiry and advocacy.[3] It's an approach that can be used by anyone—no matter his or her position—to enhance communication, improve decision-making, and develop better relationships. It's an approach that entrepreneurial leaders use almost intuitively because it creates engagement, surfaces creative ideas, and builds trust in the process.

The idea behind balancing inquiry and advocacy is to lay out your thinking and reasoning, inviting others to do the same. In effect, you are advocating your position by exposing your thinking process to others. You might communicate by saying things like "Here's what I think, and here's how I got here" or "What do you think about what I just said? Do you see any flaws in my reasoning? What can you add?" Similarly, when using inquiry to help others better articulate their reasoning, you might ask questions like "Can you help me understand your thinking here? What leads you to conclude that?" or "I'm asking about your assumptions here because . . ." Balancing inquiry and advocacy means drawing on a variety of skills—things like asserting, explaining, sensing, facilitating, and dialogue—to fully understand the facts and reasoning behind each viewpoint. But communication is not typically an end in and of itself. The entrepreneurial leader must learn to call the question after the process of exchange and advocacy.

Entrepreneurial leaders make mistakes when they think people will get the information they need without their direct communication. (Recall the saying "Nature abhors a vacuum.") They also make mistakes when they let their emotions get the better of them and respond in the heat of the moment. (This is true not only in face-to-face communications but also in email.) By responding in the heat of the moment, leaders fail to think about the potential repercussions of an angry outburst or an off-color remark.

Always remember that words aren't the only way leaders communicate. An innocent glance at the window or an unstoppable yawn will often be interpreted as boredom or disinterest; a raised eyebrow, even if the twitch is involuntary, will be seen as a sign of skepticism; a squint or the hint of an eye roll will signal disdain. For an entrepreneurial leader, communicating isn't just about choosing the right words and delivery; at other times, it's about maintaining a poker face so that inadvertent expressions don't belie your thoughts.

Although the skills of communicating can be improved over time—and implementing the mind-sets I describe will surely help—recognize that world-class communicators never stop working at it. Look at the other skills and maps in this book and recognize that every single one of them requires a leader to communicate with others. In many ways, communication is the meta skill. With that in mind, it's one you cannot spend too much time investing in to get right.

RECAP

▶ Communicate lavishly. This is best done by crisp, clear, to-the-point communications, not by long, rambling presentations that the organization will ultimately learn to ignore.

▶ Devote considerable time and energy to listening, to capturing what others are saying, to seeking input. This effort not only collects substantive help, it communicates respect.

▶ Don't plow around disappointing news. People are smart. They'll respect a leader who trusts them with the truth.

MAP 6

HOW TO RUN GREAT MEETINGS

I've left orders to be awakened at any time in case of a national emergency—even if I'm in a cabinet meeting.

—Ronald Reagan

The granular work of entrepreneurial leaders comes down to running meetings and having difficult conversations.

Every organization—business, political or nonprofit—runs on "meeting fuel." If one considers a phone call a one-on-one meeting, or a casual face-to-face conversation in the hallway an informal meeting, leaders spend most of their lives in meetings.

John Silber, the former president of Boston University, described how, initially, he was irritated by constant interruptions from students, alumni, and faculty—each wanting an audience, each with a particular agenda. When he realized that these interruptions were not *keeping* him from his work but *were* his work, he settled into a long tenure as university president. Similarly, the starting point for learning how to hold effective meetings is to appreciate them as the *sine qua non* of organizational excellence.

Since meetings are management at its grittiest level, it's surprising that many entrepreneurs, leaders, and managers are so poor at organizing them, running them, and following up on them. Hence, a modest improvement in the quality of meeting preparation, agenda generation, discussion quality, and follow-up will dramatically improve the productivity of almost any organization—and move the person in charge closer to demonstrating the skills of the most accomplished change agents, entrepreneurial leaders.

All meetings are not created equal. Some meetings are held with internal teams. Others involve customers, suppliers, shareholders, or other constituents. Some meetings, like chance encounters, just come up; others are calendared months in advance. Some are casual and free form. Others are stylized and depend on norms, rules, committees, and agendas.

Learning best practices allows one the freedom to improvise depending on circumstances. But until mastered, there's more downside in winging it than there is upside in spontaneity. Until these skills come naturally, overprepare and even rehearse how you'll lead each gathering.

You will face one pervasive challenge in holding great meetings: people at all levels of organizations have come to dislike them. This often creates a jadedness, low enthusiasm, and negative energy among those invited to meetings. That's unfortunate, given how vital they are and how much time we spend in them.

Generally speaking, these negative feelings are the result of unnecessary or poorly run meetings. If you don't immediately recognize how frequently a meeting is being poorly run, ask yourself how rarely you hear these commonsense questions asked inside your organization: How often do we *have* to meet? How long does this meeting *really* need to be? Do *all* of these people belong here? Are we clear on the purpose of this meeting? Who's going to follow up on what and by when?

Since most people bring negative emotions into meetings, it's important to counter these widely shared biases with a fresh point of view. If you view meetings as something to survive or as an organizational or bureaucratic feature to be tolerated, your attitude will quickly infect the organization. Soon those you're leading—no matter how well you do with the techniques of meeting hygiene—will vandalize every effort by every person in the organization to run an effective meeting.

Over time, I have come to believe that learning to lead great meetings requires developing two things: the right skills and the right mind-set. Both are well worth the time you will invest. Get good at holding great meetings and conversations that advance the agenda, and you'll be on your way to effective entrepreneurial leadership.

To put myself in the right mind-set, I use the following self-talk to ensure that I am entering into the work of meetings with the positive, constructive, and enthusiastic mind-set that increases the odds that the gathering will be successful:

Every meeting is a performance, not a dress rehearsal. Each one is important (and expensive)—and done well, they're a way to bond as a team and to mark milestones. I take each meeting seriously and will demonstrate that to all other attendees.

I come on time, prepared, and ready to follow up. If other members have trouble making meetings on time (and I'm chairing the meeting), I'll start on time anyway and ask them privately to help me by arriving a few minutes early next time, appealing to their sense of professionalism. As I learned at my mother's knee, "If you're not early, you're late."

I treat every conversation—by phone or in person, one-on-one or in a group—as a meeting. As such, they represent an opportunity for brand building. I regard every interaction as important, a chance to build a relationship, to understand an issue, to evaluate a set of circumstances, to make an ally. While I'll devote an appropriate amount of time, focus, and energy proportional to the importance of the issue, I also let others know ahead of time that I've only got X minutes so I don't damage our relationship by cutting off a meeting before an issue has been fully processed.

I invite feedback on meeting effectiveness. I'll follow up many formal meetings with informal discussions with participants. I want to know what we can do better and their thoughts about what went well and what didn't. I've learned to embrace negative feedback and to change my behaviors based on what I learn from these postmeeting discussions.

I want people to feel affirmed after a meeting, to feel inspired to do more and to do it better. While the business of meetings can be the serious, dry stuff of budgets, schedules, assignments, and accountability, higher performance comes from aspiring to success than fearing failure. If I can get people to see the vision, to gain a sense of what it will mean to win, I'll not only have better meetings, I'll achieve better, longer-lasting results. And I'll have a better set of meaningful relationships with the people with whom I spend so much time.

Mind-set alone won't allow a leader to become better at running meetings. You also need the right skills.

There are many excellent guides for developing better skills to lead meetings. My favorites are *Death by Meeting*[1] and *Difficult Conversations*.[2] I have relied on these books, as well as in-person coaching, to try to improve my own skills in leading meetings. I'd encourage every aspiring entrepreneurial leader to find books and informal coaching to do the same.

As in many areas of life, the mistakes people make when leading meetings tend to be well-known—but people keep right on making them anyway, every single day. Based on my years inside organizations, these are the mistakes I see most often—the ones that most frequently undermine the credibility and effectiveness of the person convening and leading the group.

1. INVITING THE WRONG PEOPLE.

Getting the right people to attend is table stakes for holding an effective meeting, yet it rarely happens. Most meetings include people who have nothing to add and/or no assignment to take out of the meeting. If people are invited simply as audience (or so they'll not feel left out), the meeting will lack focus and energy; this will squander the enthusiasm and goodwill of participants.

Everyone in attendance *must* have a focus on follow-up actions or the meeting will flop. Unless it's clear why each person is vital to the meeting, don't invite them. If the meeting covers lots of topics with relevance to various subsets of attendees, group the topics and excuse people after the topic that interests them has been handled. (Alternatively, go off-line postmeeting if an issue only involves a subset of attendees.) This imparts a message of urgency and respect for all in attendance. It also reduces the politics of "invitation comparison," in which people feel a sense of status or importance based on how many meeting invites they receive.

Jeff Bezos famously limits the size of teams by invoking the "two-pizza rule," limiting groups to only as many members as can be reasonably fed by two pies. This practice naturally reduces the number of people invited to meetings. When I plan meetings, I rely on a more succinct directive: "No audience."

2. FAILING TO PROVIDE A CLEAR FORMAT AND PURPOSE.

"Getting together to talk" almost guarantees a bad meeting. If the purpose is really to just talk, be clear about it. Right up front, tell people, "We're not going to make a decision today. We're simply going to get out all the options and generate a tentative force-ranking of action steps." This sort of lead-in will at least give clarity to the purpose of the meeting. Many leaders call meetings simply because they're unsure of themselves and want to generate cover, get others' ideas, or check their own instincts without revealing how uncertain they are. People are smart and busy. They pick up quickly on leaders who are simply assembling everyone to talk. And they tend not to like it.

Too often, meeting attendees show up not knowing exactly why they're there. If there's an agenda, send it out ahead of time. Develop and consistently use a familiar format. Let people know at the outset when the meeting will end (and stick to it). Let people know what the expected outcome of the meeting will be. Jump right into the important topic(s). State the purpose of the meeting in a single sentence at its outset. ("Today, we're going to make the decision on whether to open a new office in Detroit.") If the purpose is to make a decision, make sure you've assigned someone ahead of time to argue the counter-case to any recommendation. If *you* plan to make the decision after input, tell people you'll take into account their views but that yours will be the final call. If you plan to bring it to a vote, let people know at the outset. While process isn't the meeting king, poor process can easily get in the way of what *should be* king—that is, making good decisions that have the support of those who will execute them.

In addition to purpose, be clear about the format of the meeting, which carries with it norms around formality, expectations around participation, and how casual people should be about speaking up. For instance, a *check-in* is typically very short and routine; some teams do them standing up to emphasize brevity. ("Don't get comfortable here.") A *brainstorming meeting* will be heavily participative, focused on creative ideation, and tolerant of half-baked ideas that will be received without judgment. *Review meetings* suggest an atmosphere of constructive criticism around progress. Simply labeling a meeting correctly can help set expectations and prime participants to perform at their best.

Aside from the occasional town hall–style meeting, at which organizational information is delivered to a large group, no effective meeting should include a large number of passive attendees. One way to avoid people from falling into a passive role is to structure the agenda to ensure that everyone "makes a sound"—says something—during the first fifteen minutes of a gathering, even if it's only to raise their hands, clap, or vote on something. Engagement is key. Leaders do this by ensuring there are conflicts, dilemmas, or issues about which there can be genuine debate. (If there aren't, just send out an email with assignments.) They also manage air time: even if the purpose of the meeting requires a formal presentation, do not let it go on for longer than fifteen minutes, lest the audience tune out and become incapable of re-engaging.

3. FAILING TO MANAGE THE ATMOSPHERE AND LOGISTICS.

Humans who are hungry, tired, hot, cold, need to use the restroom, or are sitting in a room that's too loud, poorly lit, or equipped with uncomfortable seats won't achieve what they're capable of in a meeting. This sounds obvious and basic, but too many people overlook these details. Indeed, after surprisingly short periods of deprivation, people become completely unfocused. Make sure these simplest of all arrangements are taken care of—and if you have an assistant handling these details, make sure he or she recognizes how important you consider them to be.

One other logistical note: always ask "Can we meet earlier?" Organizations that hold meetings early enough in the day (and in the week) allow people time to do immediate follow-ups if necessary. End-of-day (or week) meetings (and especially those held just before a holiday) are rarely as productive as those that are convened early in the week and in the morning.

4. COMING UNPREPARED AND LEAVING WITHOUT AN ASSIGNMENT.

If people don't have to prepare anything ahead of time and feel they can walk out without any responsibility or accountability, you'll waste a lot of time and money—and, more importantly, you'll have sent a message that's hard to take back. To understand how costly meetings are, add to the hourly, fully loaded costs of the entire group the opportunity cost of holding them hostage. Then divide that number by your profit margin and you'll see the level of sales needed to justify any meeting. So if the fully loaded costs of getting twenty people together for an all-day off-site is $20,000, and your profit margin is 10 percent, you need to generate $200,000 in additional sales to cover the cost of that particular meeting. Let attendees know this number so they'll be more inclined to come prepared and leave armed to do something that justifies that level of cost.

Meetings that lack follow-up assignments quickly lead to bad habits. Remember that everything should eventually devolve into a deliverable—something that can be measured—if you're to have focus in a meeting. Quantification, where possible, imparts urgency and accountability. Reporting back on assignments not only reinforces their importance, but it also gives an opportunity to give credit to those fulfilling assignments.

5. FAILING TO MAKE MEETINGS FUN.

The use of humor, prizes, recognition, and celebration can turn the dreariness of a scheduled meeting into something fun and anticipated. Leaders naturally call meetings when things go wrong—a client defects, a major project is killed—or when they have momentous decisions to make. These gatherings should be appropriately serious. However, failing to gather people to announce good news, to celebrate great performances, to recognize individual contributors, or just to laugh together is a corollary mistake. As I indicated earlier, many people have come to dread meetings because so many of them are poorly run or a waste of time. Entrepreneurial leaders overcome that by getting people to look forward to meetings by using surprises, celebration, recognition, and fun. Some of these will be planned; others will be spontaneous. For example, one firm I know installed a gong in the reception area and rang it whenever a significant deal closed, signaling people to take a few minutes to come together to celebrate their incremental progress.

The most important way to turn meetings into a positive activity for your organization is to eliminate unnecessary ones. The good news is that you can usually avoid a bogus meeting by answering a few simple questions before you ever send out an invitation: Do we really need to meet about this? Can the invited group be smaller? Are the format and purpose clear to everyone? Is the agenda as lean as it can be, and will everyone see it in advance? This advice sounds basic, but spend time in most organizations and you will recognize how rarely it's utilized.

The payoff from asking these questions before you (or your assistant) hit SEND will be bigger than you expect. Improving your meeting culture can transform the work life of everyone on your team, including you.

You know the saying: When the outcome of a meeting is to have another meeting, it's been a lousy meeting.

RECAP

► Your effectiveness as an entrepreneurial leader will depend, to a large degree, on your effectiveness in running meetings—from board meetings to one-on-one conversations to town hall gatherings.

► Consider meetings an opportunity to train others to be on time, to expect to participate, to take on follow-up assignments, and to respect others' time.

► Don't underestimate the power of urgency, meeting hygiene, and the promise of follow-up.

MAP 7

HOW TO USE A BOARD EFFECTIVELY

A man may do an immense deal of good, if he does not care who gets the credit for it.
—Sir Mountstuart E. Grant Duff,
diary entry, September 21, 1863

Earlier in my career, when I was serving as chief financial officer, I was working extremely long hours. My youngest son, hearing me talk about the challenge of this work, and noticing how early I was leaving home in the mornings, announced that he'd never want to be a chief *financial* officer. Instead, he proposed that—unlike his old man—*he* would be a chief *executive* officer.

"Why?" I asked.

"So I don't have to report to *anyone!*" he naïvely responded.

As a child responsible for mowing the lawn, making his bed, and brushing his teeth, he longed for a job without accountability. His reckoning was that the job with the least accountability must be the one held by the person at the top of the org chart—the person to whom *everyone else* had to report.

This adolescent understanding is held by too many corner-office aspirants . . . and occupants. CEOs who see their jobs either as presidents or politicians tend to defer to board members with the most power or who represent the greatest number of votes. CEOs who see their jobs as managers tend to regard their primary duty as delivering on-time, on-budget results for projects agreed upon by a board. And CEOs who are pure entrepreneurs see boards as audiences charged with ensuring that the leader has the resources to keep the show on the road. Entrepreneurs who view the board in this way may have achieved my son's ambition—life without a boss!—but they generally fail to produce durable results or grow a sustainable business.

Entrepreneurial leaders are driven by a calculus different from that of the leaders who are pure presidents, managers, administrators, entrepreneurs, or politicians. And they thrive working with boards made up of the right people applying the cadences and principles of entrepreneurial leadership.

This suggests building a board that fits with the style of the entrepreneurial leader: one in which directors make up a constituent *team*, one that is adept at sourcing ideas, contributing the wisdom that comes from experience, and bringing a network that can contribute materially to a common objective. The board must also provide the accountability necessary for building an enduring enterprise, as well as support new initiatives that would be killed in less entrepreneurial enterprises. For this, boards must be comfortable in piloting—and in regularly sunsetting—initiatives that would be rejected in a more bureaucratic, less entrepreneurial environment.

The entrepreneurial leader working with an appropriately entrepreneurial board knows what my youngest son has realized now that he's become a CEO: everybody is accountable to somebody, and a CEO reports to the board that is elected to represent shareholders. If the CEO is lucky, she'll report to a board that works. If unlucky, she'll still have to report to one who knows less than she does but whose job is to hold her accountable. And if the leader isn't careful, she'll end up reporting to others who not only know less than she does but who criticize her every move, second-guess her every decision, get in the way of every initiative, and create their own set of politics that must be managed.

The best boards I've worked on act like owners and their members as fiduciaries. But they recognize that short-, medium-, and long-term consequences flow from their decisions. And they know that decisions have second- and third-order implications that may not be immediately apparent. Above all, they know they're there to *serve* management, *advise* them, *bring resources* to them, and *develop contingency plans*—whether for CEO succession or for economic downturns. Such directors know when to lead, when to partner, and when to stay out of the way.

The sad truth is that many boards don't do a very good job at these. For example, when preparing for downturns that are inevitable in cyclical markets, only a third of the 772 directors surveyed by McKinsey in a 2013 survey thought that the boards on which they serve understood their company's strategy. Less than a quarter were fully aware of how their firms create value, and an even smaller percentage thought they understood the dynamics of their firms' industries.

This means that dysfunctional boards tend to be either *ceremonial*, simply rubber-stamping management's plans, or *activist*, meddling in every operating decision, creating strife-filled politics that taint every decision. Toxic boards that act as "the parsley on the fish" or as activist, agenda-driven, "pain-in-the-neck" watchdogs are not helpful in building long-term value—a board's key job.

But it's not just bad director behavior for which the entrepreneurial leader must be on the lookout. I once served on the board of a bank that no longer exists. Essentially, I and twenty-three other directors sat in rows—schoolroom style—to watch bankers make presentations for a half day every quarter. We were audience, they were actors; the whole thing was a farce. They controlled the agenda, the pacing, the follow-up. After two meetings, I resigned. While this was a particularly ineffective board, the truth is that of the thirty-six boards on which I've served, almost a third of them haven't worked much better.

If an entrepreneurial leader is saddled with bad directors, it's time to reorganize the board, get training for directors, or find a new job. Otherwise, debilitating questions of authority will arise and dangerous meddling in day-to-day operations will eventually imperil the firm.

When entrepreneurial leaders recognize that certain directors or certain processes are destroying value, they must initiate change—both in board composition and in board process. Above all, entrepreneurial leaders must be committed to getting the right set of advisors talking about the right set of issues and then acting consistently with best governance practices.

Even though the CEO reports to the board, making sure the board is working effectively is partly the responsibility of the entrepreneurial leader as CEO. Failing to recognize this, leaders will find themselves dreading board meetings. And when that happens, customers, investors, and employees all lose.

What follows are some of the rules I've learned to follow when building a board, serving on a board, reporting to a board, or advising or chairing a board. As with most maps in this book, they represent time- and experience-tested rules worthy of consideration by anyone who would be an entrepreneurial leader.

The first issue to consider is how to *build* a high-quality board in the first place. Best practices for the entrepreneurial leader who has some level of control over building the board include:

1. At the time you're raising capital, patiently assemble a company's initial board—one you expect to outgrow as the company develops.
2. Ask potential investors for candidates to serve as board members, and don't assume that the biggest investors will be the best board members.
3. Remember that a board is a team. Select for those who "play well with others," know how to listen, and have high

emotional intelligence, or EQ. If you don't, you'll be refereeing disputes, soothing egos, and wasting time.

4. Consider splitting the CEO and chairman roles. If you don't split them, make sure you have a lead director to work with independent directors on succession planning, executive sessions, and issues that involve management evaluation, coaching, and feedback.

5. Get and provide references. When selecting a board, you're solving for "fit." Board candidates should be interviewing you as much as you're interviewing them. Unless both parties make a good all-things-considered decision, you're in for misery.

6. Move slowly and carefully. Adding board members is easier than removing them.

7. As you expand the board, consider using outside search firms to source and screen candidates—both for expertise and for cultural fit.

8. Set up onboarding and off-boarding rules that include term limits, age limits, self- and third party–assessments. Do this before people lock in to board service.

9. Have the governance and nominating committee do an annual review of each board member and set up the expectation that people will cycle off the board at reasonable intervals.

10. Be wary of selecting for functional expertise. Although it can be helpful to have someone with particularly relevant experience, you mustn't confuse deep experience or expertise with being a good board member. Board members bring all-things-considered wisdom that can be applied to any functional expertise. You can rent expertise à la carte.

11. Use compensation consultants to determine board pay. Then pay for board service and expect preparation—and real value— from each board member.

The next issue for the effective entrepreneurial leader to consider is how to *organize* board meetings:

1. Suggest and agree upon norms for attendance, whether in person or by phone.

2. Provide for adequate breaks and have rules about the usage of electronics. Set these up *before* there's a problem.

3. Commit to sending out board materials three to five days in advance of the board meeting. Assume directors have read the material.

4. Be mindful of airtime—boards are not audiences, so facilitate discussion, cold-calling if necessary.

5. Set up standing committees (compensation, audit, governance) and have them report to the full board at each meeting.

6. Set thirty minutes aside at the end of the meeting for an executive session in which the CEO leaves the room so independent directors can discuss openly CEO performance, identify unaddressed questions, and make recommendations for the next meeting. The lead director or chairman directs this discussion.

7. Have the lead director or chairman monitor norms, structure, and processes and suggest remedial action to the entire board; codevelop with the CEO all agenda items in advance of every meeting, making sure the focus stays on value drivers; serve as CEO coach; and work on board development by recruiting new directors (working closely with the governance and nominating committee).

8. Schedule your quarterly in-person board meetings a year in advance to allow members to plan ahead. Pick locations near hub airports, and optimize both location and schedule for in-person attendance and efficiency. Schedule meetings early enough in the day that people can fly home the same day. Be strategic about dinners and

social time, recognizing that they can build the fabric of the board and provide time outside of the agenda. Between board meetings, convene by phone when necessary. The best entrepreneurial leaders provide their board members a hassle-free experience and expose them to key elements of the operation.

9. Don't overload the agenda. Focus on requisite administrative, urgent, and timely matters, adding to them a topic to address in depth. Covering all aspects of the business—at every meeting—will frustrate directors, exhaust staff, and leave little time for discussion, which is the reason to have a board in the first place. Start with the most important topics. Don't save the most critical topics for the end, when the energy is lowest and the airport is beckoning.

10. Keep minutes concise. They're not intended to provide a detailed description of everything that was discussed during the meeting. Keep in mind that minutes are discoverable in litigation. Make them litigation proof. Generally speaking, less is more.

During my many years of board service, I have seen the same mistakes made over and over—poor practices which reduce the effectiveness of directors and make meetings less valuable than they might otherwise be. Here are some practices to avoid:

- **Mistake #1**—Treating the board meeting like a presentation. Assume board members are up to speed on the status of the company and ready to add value. Forcing them to sit through hours in silence as you flip through PowerPoint slides will kill discussion.
- **Mistake #2**—Rereading the report to your board rather than assuming everyone has read the material. If you use board materials as a presentation crutch, you'll burn up precious

minutes walking page-by-page through information that your board should have already processed on their own time.

- **Mistake #3**—Talking too much rather than facilitating discussion. CEOs who talk at their boards too much wind up with directors who perceive themselves as a compliance requirement rather than servants dedicated to helping you run your business.

- **Mistake #4**—Responding to every comment or, worse, failing to bring in every board member, even by cold-calling, to share their experience. You're looking for dialogue, for discussion, for debate.

- **Mistake #5**—Failing to use your board members outside of meetings via one-on-one conversations. These conversations often add more value than what happens in the regular meeting. In many instances, directors have expertise that can help with a specific problem that isn't worth taking time from a board meeting to discuss.

- **Mistake #6**—Failing to track open items from each meeting and following up either between meetings or at the beginning of the following meeting.

- **Mistake #7**—Avoiding the delivery of bad news. All companies have ups and downs. Bad stuff happens. Don't surprise the board. Deliver bad news with as much clarity as you celebrate good news. Entrepreneurial leaders—just like presiders, managers, administrators, entrepreneurs, and politicians—make mistakes. The best of them are simply better at learning from them than are their counterparts.

Boards can supercharge an enterprise or drag it down. Some rubber-stamp whatever management wants to do. Others get in the way. Some spend time on the agendas or idiosyncrasies of individual directors. It's partly the CEO's responsibility to make sure the board doesn't fall into that trap—and that it is adding value by ensuring the enterprise is led by the right people, following best practices for governance, and using their own contacts, perspectives, and wisdom to help a management team benefit from their experience.

RECAP

- ▶ A board can either add value or destroy a company. Directors must work together as a team, understand their duties of care and loyalty to shareholders, and hold management accountable while serving as a resource.

- ▶ Boards must be assembled with an eye not just toward functional competencies but also for judgment, wisdom, and courage.

- ▶ There are best practices for board development, meetings, and follow-up. Set norms at the outset, "socialize" issues prior to the meeting, and follow the rules for building an agenda and running a board meeting.

MAP 8

HOW TO OVERCOME ADVERSITY

I have no fear of the future. Let us go forward into its mysteries, let us tear aside the veils which hide it from our eyes, and let us move onward with confidence and courage.

—Winston Churchill, in a speech at
Royal Albert Hall, London,
September 29, 1943

Setbacks are in your future. Entrepreneurial leaders recognize that. They may simply run into "bad weather" in the form of an aggressive competitive response, a bad economy, or unexpected difficulty with suppliers, distributors, or creditors. Of course, the fault may be their own bad decisions, fumbling an execution, or suffering a betrayal by someone they trusted.

Based on my airline industry experience, when nothing is going well, I've found it helpful to remember that it's always sunny above the clouds. Gaining a bit of altitude changes everything. A similar image has seen me through some of my darker moments when I've realized that, at every moment of every day, somewhere in the world it is daybreak. If I can survive the night, the world will look different when dawn breaks. Likewise, in a turnaround, a change of perspective can do wonders.

A full-blown turnaround is a big deal for any business leader. For entrepreneurs reluctant to initiate surgery to preserve a business they founded, it's often the end of the road. Entrepreneurial leaders are invariably optimists who tend to believe in the business (even when the facts don't support their optimism). They're probably responsible for some of its most serious problems.

And because most entrepreneurs are the spark and source of ideas and inspiration, they tend to be all about new products, new services, new customers, and growth. In a turnaround, those considerations need to take a back seat to an exigency—surviving a dark night on the mountain. That often requires cutting back, consolidating, and fixing systems.

Here's where entrepreneurial leaders shine. Unlike the pure entrepreneur, they are able to shift gears and focus on consolidating instead of growing, not only doing the job better than pure entrepreneurs but better than "professional managers." Entrepreneurial leaders use this critical—and predictable—stage in the lifecycle to build an institution that is better and stronger for having faced and survived a crisis.

The best turnarounds are quiet and undramatic because they happen incrementally over time—think, of course, corrections instead of violent U-turns. Just as changing one's diet and exercise patterns would improve one's health, many dramatic enterprise changes won't feel like turnarounds if done incrementally and with discipline. Indeed, the aim should be to ensure there's never a need for the sort of intervention that puts the business at risk in order to save it.

I've found six smart steps for managing a turnaround.

1. CONFRONT REALITY.

The failure to recognize trends, to understand underlying changes in the market, and to evaluate competitive threats represent a denial of reality. Continuing the status quo and failing to recognize emerging threats is a pattern in every business decline. Successful turnarounds start with embracing reality. This means embracing bad news, shining a light in dark corners, and asking questions.

Entrepreneurial leaders who do well with turnarounds are honest in their assessment of the challenges facing the organization. They may bring in fresh eyes to help them understand problems. They don't sugarcoat the truth, and they are not afraid of delivering bad news. They understand that denying reality is toxic to a turnaround effort and will almost certainly lead to failure.

No one ever has all the information they need to predict future events. One of the mind-sets effective entrepreneurial leaders bring is an admission of vulnerabilities and an acknowledgement of what they don't know. If you're leading a turnaround and don't know the answers to key questions, don't fake it.

2. IDENTIFY THE TEAM.

When facing hardship, entrepreneurial leaders pull all of the key leaders into the tent. They commit to transparency and open, honest communication. They get commitment to see things through to a specific target. The level of trust necessary to do this had better have been built *before* the crisis. Indeed, the most important asset a leader will have in a turnaround is the trust of those whose help he or she needs—both inside and outside the enterprise.

Turnarounds are a team effort, and success depends on everyone pulling together. Therefore, it is critical to identify your core team early on—who should stay and who you should let go to conserve resources. Your A team should help to form your game plan.

A turnaround can be an opportunity for people to shine—to show their capabilities under duress. It can also be an opportunity to form a highly cohesive team. In my own career, the best thing that ever happened to me was an industry meltdown shortly after I started work.

Although the challenges in a turnaround are significant, skillful leaders create a context in which people bond together, rise to the occasion, take responsibility, and feel empowered to do remarkable work together. A good metaphor for how the team must work together is that of a climbing team belayed on a cliff. If they are to make it to the top, they will need to trust each other and work together. They will each be dependent on the others for survival. Entrepreneurial leaders put together teams they trust and inspire them to believe that, collectively, they can prevail. They portray the situation as an adventure—one that will help the organization learn and become stronger.

Unfortunately, most turnarounds require leaders to reduce the workforce. When this is necessary, it is best to do so quickly and humanely. It is up to the leader to define the reality and explain that if the organization is to survive, it must shrink its labor costs quickly. This is best done early, when there are still resources for generous severance; if you put off downsizing until later, far more people may suffer, and the organization's ability to survive may be weakened beyond repair.

3. FOCUS ON THE CORE.

The good news is that many turnarounds can be achieved simply by stopping what isn't working. This can be relatively painless if done soon enough and regularly enough. Often there are pockets of a business that are doing well and would be thriving if they weren't attached to those that are struggling. Simply selling off or shutting down what isn't working may be the best way to execute a relatively quick turnaround. Analyzing what it would mean to cut noncore activities—and by doing so, eliminating nonessentials that are consuming capital, distracting people, and absorbing time—is a first step.

The turnarounds that require no more than arresting certain unprofitable activities are theoretically the easiest to execute; however, all activities have supporters who may be among the more politically powerful, complicating the "best idea wins" principle of turnaround management.

Another so-called easy fix is across-the-board cuts. However, this fair-sounding approach is generally another recipe for failure. The better way to cut costs is to start with analyzing what are the costs *necessary* for delivery of core products and services. What can we not do without and still meet our mission? is the question you should be asking. Zero-based, ground-up budgeting should start immediately. The government formula of scaling back built-in increases is just another recipe for failure.

In most cases, successful turnarounds require more than cost cutting. Entrepreneurial leaders must also formulate a *recovery plan* specifying the strategic direction that will lead the company back to sustained profitability. To do that, leaders have to evaluate what caused the organization's downturn in the first place. If they don't develop an accurate assessment, it's unlikely they'll develop an appropriate recovery plan. As part of this evaluation process, it's important to assess the relative roles of operational inefficiency and strategic misalignment as they've contributed to the company's financial decline.

A well-defined retrenchment and recovery plan reduces anxiety among team members. Without a plan, people look out for themselves. With a plan to which they're committed, they spend time on activities that advance the business and speed recovery.

4. SET METRICS.

Having clear and limited goals is *always* important—but never more so than in a turnaround. Most turnarounds require resetting priorities. Invariably this short list will all be about survival. When I was doing this at Trammell Crow Company, our metrics focused on liquidity, inventory levels, rental revenues, and debt levels. These became *job one*—against which every division was measured. Later we would set profitability goals; and later still, well-run goals around best practices, financial disciplines, and so on. Unless everyone can remember what winning is, you've not done a good job at setting survival objectives.

As noted in the section on creating MAD goals, unless you set measurable metrics with (1) time frames, (2) budgets, (3) champions, and (4) deliverables, you don't have a goal—you have a wish. Entrepreneurial leaders establish simple *dashboards* with key metrics to track and signal progress.

Turnarounds are almost always related to financial strength, which is a function of the company's balance sheet, income statement, and funds flow. As a result, entrepreneurial leaders create easy-to-follow monitoring systems—or dashboards—by selecting one or two specific metrics reflecting each financial indicator. The goal is to select metrics that represent key drivers of the organization's performance. In general, it's a good idea to select a revenue target and cost reduction targets to include in your dashboard. You should also try to include at least one leading indicator for each. Leading indicators are important because they allow leaders to look ahead. Many managers don't pay a lot of attention to leading indicators when things are going well. As a result, they miss opportunities to foresee and head off potential problems. The sales pipeline is a good example of a leading indicator. Whatever you choose, make sure they're posted and success is celebrated.

5. EXTEND THE RUNWAY.

In the first phase of a turnaround, it's all about cash. Entrepreneurial leaders do everything possible to secure the working capital needed to keep the organization running and to fund the turnaround effort for however long is necessary.

There are a number of ways to build up cash balances during the early stages of a turnaround. These include extending payables, advancing receivables (by accelerating the sales cycle or closing more quickly, perhaps by discounting), liquidating assets, or taking the obvious steps (like head count reductions) to pare expenses.

Timing and discipline are important. When beginning a turnaround, it's a good idea to determine what the company can realistically afford. What is the minimum level of cash below which you cannot operate? What are the bare bone costs of running the organization from a financial perspective? Once these are determined, the operations team has to determine what must be cut—or looked at differently—to conduct business at these lower limits.

If you're out of cash, you're out of business. Cash is the cushion businesses need to make the changes necessary to preserve themselves. If sales decline, margins compress, or costs spike, businesses need to preserve cash, building up a war chest until the peril is understood and dealt with. Without sufficient liquidity, a business cannot reorganize. Some inexperienced entrepreneurs underestimate the need for liquidity and neglect to begin a workout regimen before it's too late. Wise entrepreneurial leaders recognize they're in trouble before they don't have adequate liquidity to see them through a turnaround and reorganization.

Indeed, extending the cash runway is a vital ingredient in any turnaround manual—but it must be done with a plan to actually turn things around, one marked by milestones of achievement. Without a plan with milestones, there is no point in simply deferring the inevitable. Extending the runway simply to delay the day of reckoning is irresponsible and will only make the problem thornier as time goes on.

6. TAKE ACTION NOW.

Sometimes management teams look for a "good" time to take on the turnaround. In reality, there will never be a good time. The best time is yesterday. Putting off what is unpleasant until it is obvious to all is to secure failure. Overanalyzing and failing to iterate quickly and reverse course all contribute to the severity of problems and the aggressiveness of the eventual turnaround.

During my time at Trammell Crow Company, we engaged in costly dithering. The facts were clear (or should have been). We were growing too fast. We were overleveraged. Markets were softening. The tax law was changing. We had an internal economy set up with free guarantees on third-party debt, cheap intercompany loans, low salaries, and below-market internal fees for managing our existing asset base. It was a formula for exactly what we got—the fastest-growing real estate development company in the nation, the largest contingent of young (on paper) millionaires per capita of any business, and a boundless optimism in the face of gathering storm clouds. In retrospect, I recognized signs of trouble early, but I failed to gather data and prove the case to my colleagues, so my efforts to course correct were thwarted. Looking back, I wish I'd begun making the case for a significant course correction earlier, more loudly, and more convincingly. Indeed, I've come to see that every well-managed business led by an entrepreneurial leader is already implementing several turnaround principles.

Inevitably, entrepreneurial leaders will face rough patches. When they do, attitude is everything.

Leading an organization through a turnaround takes an emotional toll, even if the outcome is positive. Entrepreneurial leaders will minimize this toll if they focus not only on the levers they must pull to right the ship but on having the right mind-set for this taxing work.

The right mind-set includes trying to avoid the natural fear of failure. Keep in mind that the lessons one learns by leading through adversity will last a lifetime. Recognize that although some may be tempted to assign blame for what's gone wrong, there's little upside to personalizing the causes of an organization's decline. Finding scapegoats is rarely a profitable activity.

The right mind-set also recognizes the very painful steps you will be required to take. Every turnaround requires layoffs and firing people. Most people who lose their jobs in a turnaround were not responsible for the problems the business is facing; therefore, you should work hard to ensure the best possible outcomes for everyone involved. As you make these difficult moves, promise yourself: *We will honor our dead and wounded by treating them with generosity and respect.*

To those who are left on the team, recognize that even in a turnaround, people need occasional reasons to celebrate wins. Therefore, setting achievable objectives like "lose less money this quarter than we lost last quarter" or "developing a line of business or a product where we are clearly winning" is important to morale. It is important not only to celebrate the successes in budget cuts, reworking liabilities, and reducing head count but also to recognize areas for growth. Failing to define a future while everyone is so busy saving the present can leave people so exhausted that the company stalls out after the turnaround is complete.

Finally, recognize the need for personal strength and self-care. Turn-arounds are tough, physically and emotionally. One of the most difficult hardships entrepreneurial leaders face when managing a turnaround is isolation. Seek out trusting relationships with external confidants. It can be comforting to talk with people who not only have your best interests at heart but who have also led a turnaround of their own. You can develop these relationships by reaching out to people during their times of struggle. If you spend a long career in business, nearly everyone will experience this feeling, and they will appreciate the company.

RECAP

▶ Adversity tests teams, builds strength, forces creativity, and can, if well managed, increase esprit de corps.

▶ Turnaround principles are nothing more than good management under duress, and entrepreneurial leaders apply the same disciplines before problems are acute.

▶ Failure is not the worst outcome of a turnaround. Giving up before you need to or giving in to breaches of trust are worse and can be fatal to your brand.

MAP 9

HOW TO
SURVIVE
GROWTH

All growth depends upon activity. There is no develop-
ment physically or intellectually without effort, and effort
means work.
　　　　　—Calvin Coolidge, quoted in *Adequate Brevity:*
　　　　　　　　　Mental Processes of Calvin Coolidge (1924)

G eoffrey West is a theoretical physicist who, according to his online biography, has spent much of his career studying "elementary particles, their interactions, and cosmological implications."[1] But in his 2017 book *Scale*, West expanded his lens to study a very different type of living thing: social organizations such as cities and corporations.

Like living organisms, companies grow and evolve—and eventually, most die. Indeed, it's rare for companies to last for centuries. Many can't even last for multiple decades. In his book, West and his team of researchers laboriously calculated the longevity of different cohorts of companies. "Companies are surprisingly biological and from an evolutionary perspective their mortality is an important ingredient for generating innovative vitality resulting from 'creative destruction' and 'the survival of the fittest,'" West writes. "Just as all organisms must die in order that the new and novel may blossom, so it is that all companies disappear or morph to allow new innovative variations to flourish: better to have the excitement and innovation of a Google or Tesla than the stagnation of a geriatric IBM or General Motors."[2] West's calculations, for instance, show that of the 28,853 companies whose stock has traded on public markets since 1950, 22,469 (or 78 percent) had died by 2009—roughly half of the "deaths" happening when the company merged or was acquired by another firm.[3]

Thus growth and maturation are an inevitable part of every organization's evolution. Entrepreneurial leaders understand that organizations, like people, have a natural life cycle and that transitions from one stage to the next, though inevitable, are also difficult. And as West's research makes clear, most firms eventually die off, either filing for bankruptcy or being acquired by another company.

For entrepreneurial leaders, recognizing that a company's growth comes in predictable chunks is essential, because managing the transitions between stages is a crucial task. Managerial practices that work well during one phase of a company's evolution become entirely unsuitable for sustaining its growth into the next phase. Periods of growth can be particularly challenging because they require leaders to grapple with a number of thorny issues, such as rapidly increasing complexity, seemingly impossible trade-offs that can define or destroy an organization's culture, and growing scrutiny in the face of new regulations or resource requirements.

The late Larry Greiner, who was a professor at the University of Southern California, conducted what is widely considered to be the classic work on the dynamics of organizational growth. Drawing on numerous organizational case studies, Greiner concluded that organizations typically progress through a somewhat predictable life cycle comprising six distinct developmental phases of growth. Each growth phase begins with a period of prolonged growth and stability, which Greiner called "evolution," and ends with a period of turmoil and change, which he labeled "a crisis." For instance, in Greiner's fourth phase, a firm experiences "growth through coordination" as a more robust management system allows managers to provide better guidance to the variety of activities going on in the firm, and this more efficient system helps power company growth. Coordination is good only up to a point, however, and in Greiner's model, the "growth through coordination" phase typically ends when the firm experiences the "crisis of red tape"—meaning that coordination has become so excessive that it's now experienced as an oppressive and counterproductive bureaucracy.[4]

Ichak Adizes, former professor at UCLA, Stanford, and Tel Aviv University, has written extensively (twenty-six books) with a slightly different optic on what he calls the "corporate life cycle." In each stage—from infancy to old age—the enterprise is exposed to mortality, much as we are as humans. And the patterns and perils are just as predictable. In a course I teach at Stanford, we examine the most common challenges leaders face at each stage.

During a company's critical early transitions, Adizes notes that the five most common fatal diseases have to do with (1) hiring mistakes, (2) illiquidity, (3) a failure of cultural norms, (4) an unwillingness to evolve in response to changing market needs, and (5) what Adizes refers to as the "founder's trap."

The founder's trap occurs when an organization is outgrowing its existing capabilities. The company is becoming too big to function with the entrepreneur at the center of all decisions. It's past the stage Adizes calls the go-go period and entering what he and other researchers refer to as a company's adolescence. (I've always thought he selected this term because it's the stage where companies are clumsy, tripping over their own feet, and suffering from systems and people that no longer fit the job at hand.) While pure entrepreneurs are vital to get through the go-go phase, the transition into and beyond adolescence requires additional help, often in the form of professional managers who can create a more systematic way for the company to do its business. The founder's trap happens when founders resist these moves; they begin to feel their "baby" has been kidnapped by an interloper, creating a dangerous passage (and often, a governance crisis) that kills many fledgling companies.

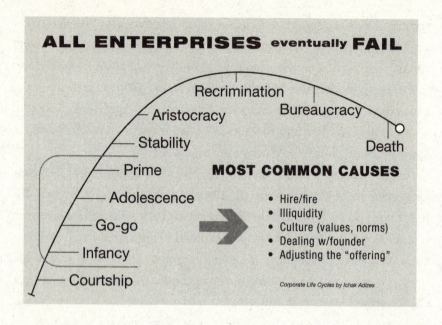

Boards tend to want to hire a fresh set of management eyes during adolescence because it's a challenging transition. They also recognize that founder-only leaders don't generally do surgery on themselves, change their teams, or replace the systems that have so far succeeded. Moreover, they are generally loath to give up the reins.

While most founders find this transition threatening, others find it frightening. A few even find it boring. But almost all worry that systems, processes, standards, and so-called best practices will kill the entrepreneurial spirit that accounts for present success. Thus pure entrepreneurs typically resist what they refer to as managers, administrators, "number crunchers," or presiders. Introducing them too early creates conflict and can even cause old ways to break down prematurely. Suddenly, out of growth—one measure of early success— the risk of failure appears. Not only do systems fail, but people who were perfect for an earlier stage find they're unable to keep up with size, complexity, or unfamiliar challenges.

Getting out of the founder's trap—or beyond the mind-set of the pure entrepreneur—often requires an intervention. This is where a wise board can be invaluable. But interventions are dangerous and if not done carefully, sequentially, and with cooperation from the founder, they can trigger a premature death.

Learning how to survive a meteoric rise without taking a precipitous fall is one measure of an entrepreneurial leader.

The biggest mistakes I've made in my forty-five years in business have come when exuberance from growth masked the seeds of the urgent need for consolidation. Many of the wisest entrepreneurial leaders I know will voluntarily cut back on growth to ensure sustainability. Others will use moments of rapid growth to sort through customers to retain only the best. Still others will use periods of growth to attract new talent, upgrade systems, and address struggling teams.

Since entrepreneurs instinctively drive for growth, it can be difficult to recognize how growth creates risks—along with opportunities. Among the signals that growth may pose a risk are:

1. Early-stage employees may be unable to keep up.
2. Expenses increase faster than revenue, in many cases because of "hobbies"—activities that are outside the core mission of the company but begin as small projects and take on a life of their own.
3. High growth attracts competitors.
4. Operational problems, in such areas as supply chain and information management, arise.
5. Cash becomes tight.

When a company starts experiencing these symptoms, it means that growth may be creating a threat. I think of these signs like a medical test. Once you have a diagnosis, you recognize the specific steps you can take to alleviate the symptoms. These include:

Replace early-stage employees (even founders) while the company is still growing. Smart leaders can tell when team members are being stretched beyond their capabilities and performance is deteriorating. In high-growth organizations, financial growth always exceeds talent growth. If a leader allows this to continue, the organization will be at risk. Leaders minimize this problem by anticipating it, establishing it at the outset as a cultural norm (including for yourself), and letting everyone know that the organization will make changes when necessary. (Refer back to the sections of this book on hiring and firing—you will do both frequently when leading a high-growth company.)

When scaling organizations, many can't afford to pay the market rate for the talent they need; they overcome this by emphasizing mission and using equity compensation to offset limited cash. The thorniest people issues involve a founder or early CEO whose talents are not keeping pace with the company's growth. This happens most frequently for pure entrepreneurs who are not making the transition to become an entrepreneurial leader—a death sentence in a high-growth organization. Founders and CEOs are subject to the same rules as everyone else, and when it's time for them to leave, they must put the interests of the enterprise and its shareholders above all else, and do so with grace.

Create rules for sunsetting unfocused initiatives. Growth allows companies to get sloppy, to say yes to projects that aren't essential and probably won't grow to be substantial. Over time, these hobbies can drain profits. To avoid that, make a list of every project, pilot, experiment, or initiative. (When we did this at one company I worked with, we found thirty-five such projects—far too many.) Identify which are related to the core and show a path to become substantial and profitable. Kill the rest—and make sure the organization becomes disciplined about systematically culling pilots to refocus on sustainable growth.

Anticipate margin compression. High profits are bound to attract competitors. When that happens, existing players will see margins shrink. Smart leaders plan ahead and are continually seeking ways to maintain or improve their product's unique advantages, increase customer loyalty, and counteract margin compression. Some companies have a moat that limits competition; others may enjoy a longer-than-usual period before competitors notice the growth they are experiencing. Even in these situations, it's essential to prepare for new entrants and increased competition. It's coming, sooner or later. Live by the mind-set made famous by Intel CEO Andy Grove, who titled his well-received 2010 book *Only the Paranoid Survive.*

Think systematically and holistically. Most companies outgrow their infrastructure, whether it's manufacturing, data, accounting systems, or the connection between all of them. Joy Covey, the former CFO of Amazon (now deceased), described the problem this way: "For Amazon, when we hit $1 billion in sales, nothing worked anymore. The wheels came off all of our systems."[5] Upgrading these systems (particularly if they are connected) can take far longer and cost much more than you expect. Pay attention to this before it becomes a full-blown crisis. Hire people who've worked in similar industries and scaled companies through this stage. Talk to vendors to become knowledgeable about options before you need them. Even when cash is tight, it can pay to have extra capacity in systems.

Make sure you have access to cash. In growth, cash comes under pressure. A growing company is making capital investments. Rising sales means rising receivables, stretching working capital. Short of organizational surgery, the three most common ways a company can get more cash are: (1) stretching payables, (2) advancing the collection of receivables (perhaps using discounts), or (3) raising capital. Managing payables and receivables is part of disciplined financial management. Raising capital is so essential that Map 4 in this book focused exclusively on it. Smart entrepreneurial leaders raise cash before they need it, even if it means parting with equity they'd prefer to keep. They hold a larger cash cushion than they may obviously need, and they look at their income statements using what-if scenarios, assessing how a negative change in a key variable might negatively affect the inflow or outflow of cash. Companies that wait until they have just a few months cash at their current burn rate before starting to raise more are imperiling the enterprise.

One of the class sessions I teach at Stanford focuses on turnarounds. We tend to think of companies in need of turnaround as older, lumbering dinosaurs—companies like General Motors or General Electric. In fact, the need for a turnaround can be triggered by a variety of factors: a declining market, poor management, or product obsolescence.

Ironically, growth can also create the problems that lead to the need for a turnaround—and the problems of growth tend to be ones that many leaders fail to recognize as a risk. In class, several of the companies we discuss that require a turnaround are early stage. In my work as an investor and board member, I routinely see companies just past the start-up stage that are experiencing nice growth. The lucky ones are led by entrepreneurial leaders who know that growth is a condition in which the seeds of problems are planted—and they get ahead of them early.

RECAP

▶ Every entrepreneurial leader desires growth, but growth comes with risk—in particular, for system breakdowns, financial strains, and organizational stress.

▶ Organizations, like humans, go through predictable stages of growth. In the "toddler to adolescent" stages, the risks are more acute than in later stages. Recognizing the specific risks at each stage of growth make them easier to manage.

▶ The potentially fatal founder's trap usually raises its ugly head when growth outstrips existing systems, personnel, and structure.

MAP 10

HOW TO DRIVE CHANGE

All is flux, nothing stands still.
—Heraclitus, from *Lives of Eminent Philosophers*,
Book IX, section 8

The primary job of the entrepreneurial leader is to prompt, inspire, and measure change, often spotting the need for *transformational* change before many would see any need to change course. This means that entrepreneurial leaders often see around corners, recognize patterns, and solve problems before they become urgent. By contrast, many other leaders and managers tend to spend more time planning and implementing incremental changes—and trying to prod slow-moving, bureaucratic organizations to go along with them.

Executives in large organizations often have a harder time engineering change than do those leading smaller organizations. Thus large organizations are often led by those with a greater tendency to create cultures in which failure is punished, complexity rewarded, and celebrations for risk taking rare.

All change should be approached with some trepidation. However, so should avoiding change. While Churchill reminds us that "to improve is to change, so to be perfect is to have changed often,"[1] Mary Shelley (author of *Frankenstein*) observed that "nothing is so painful to the human mind as great and sudden change."[2] Both cautions are true. But it's worth noting that most people tend to hold back, fearing implications of the unknown.

While it would be foolish to take change lightly, effective entrepreneurial leaders know three things about change:

1. Anyone can be a change agent if they approach it intentionally and systematically.
2. Once teams determine a change is in their interest, the transformation can't be stopped.
3. Change agents must model behavior, not just talk about it.

Entrepreneurial leaders have learned that it's not so much that people are afraid of change as it is that they instinctively resist *mandated* change, illustrating the vital role trust plays when recruiting team members to author changes they'll get behind. This means the first step to becoming an entrepreneurial leader—building a brand for high trust—will be the foundation upon which becoming an agent of durable change can be built.

In the mid-2000s, Arthur Brooks would not have fit anyone's conception of a change agent. Prior to becoming president of the American Enterprise Institute in 2009, there was almost nothing in Brooks's past that could have suggested he had the capacity to drive change. He'd spent his twenties as a professional French horn player, completed his college degree through a correspondence program, and then spent years as a tenured professor at Syracuse. Nonetheless, his books—including *Gross National Happiness* and *Who Really Cares*—illustrated his ability to think innovatively and to take intellectual risks. Based on his published works and on his powerful personal presence, AEI's board saw that even if his résumé was unconventional, Brooks had the potential to transform their organization.

By any measure, Brooks revolutionized AEI by taking a systematic approach to policy development and fund-raising. Like most good leaders,

Brooks has an obsession with measuring progress. AEI is a think tank, so its output is hard-to-quantify ideas. Nonetheless, Brooks began measuring AEI's output in terms of op-eds published, media invitations and interviews, and Congressional testimony provided, comparing those metrics with those of competing think tanks. Rather than throw AEI's ideas out into a vague, undefined "market," Brooks offered a clear strategy for how the organization would propagate its ideas. This was based on a segmentation of the four different types of people who might see AEI's work: *true believers* (who already agree with AEI's views), *persuadables* (who are open to hearing from AEI), *hostiles* (who think AEI's perspective is stupid), and *apathetics* (who don't care). To maximize its impact, AEI crosses these classifications against targets in the media, in Congress, in business, and in the nonprofit world. Much like a salesforce sizes up prospects based on their potential return-on-investment, Brooks trained AEI to maximize its impact by focusing its message on the most influential and persuadable audiences. Using this approach has also reinvigorated its fund-raising.[3]

In 2018, when Brooks announced he was leaving AEI the following year, he was recognized not only as an influential guru and advisor to leading conservative politicians but as a leader who had helped to dramatically increase AEI's standing in Washington and beyond. During a decade in the job, he transformed that organization.

Often the first step in being a change agent is to make sure you've changed your own operating system to make sure it's an effective one. Once you've done that, you can begin to try to change an organization, as Arthur Brooks did.

History is filled with examples of unlikely change agents, including Harry Truman, Abraham Lincoln, Ulysses S. Grant, and Alexander Hamilton. Their biographies remain compelling, in part, because of how each of them first changed himself and then changed the nation.

Change agents recognize that transformation depends on more than themselves. They recruit allies and convince people that change is in their interest—and that failing to change may prove perilous.

For Bob Whitman, CEO of Franklin Covey, the ability to drive change also began with self-transformation. Early in his career, Bob had a simple worldview: when a problem pops up, it's the boss's job to solve it, usually by himself. During the real estate crash of the late 1980s, however, when Bob was chief financial officer of Trammell Crow Company, he began to recognize that this mind-set was no longer serving him well. "I had to recognize that these people were all partners—they were some of the most capable real estate people in the world, powerful guys who'd built large and very successful businesses,"[4] he says. Instead of supplying the answer to them, Bob began to treat them as equals who would collaborate with him to find a solution together. Instead of imposing change, he began presenting the team with a problem, urging them to collaborate to devise the necessary solutions.

That approach continues to this day. "When you see yourself as the genius with a thousand helpers, as the person who needs to think up all the ideas, that translates into a specific kind of leadership," Bob says. Typically, it means a hierarchical, top-down, formal culture. "If you realize that genius lies in the extremely capable people you've hired, then the leader's job isn't to generate all the ideas—it's to set up an environment that gets the best ideas out of them, by giving them autonomy and authority within a framework."[5] That's a very different approach—and, over time, a better way to drive durable change.

Trying to lead an organization through a dramatic change can be daunting. One way to overcome the trepidation is to break a long journey into a series of shorter trips. Keep the summit in mind but focus on the path you want to take and the distance you want to go a day at a time. Changing directions is easier than imagining the entire journey; and incremental progress—one step and one mile at a time—can give people a sense of accomplishment and reduce the anxiety they may feel about the scope of the transformation. Think big, but start small.

Just as change agents need to recruit like-minded allies, they must also keep an eye out for blockers—people who are not just resistant to the change but who actively try to rally others to protect the status quo. When a change agent identifies such people, he should engage and start a dialogue to try to understand the roots of their resistance. And if that proves unproductive, they should find a means to part ways. The path to a new summit is hard enough without carrying dead weight—or worse, those pulling in an opposite direction.

People fear and avoid change for several reasons. Among them are inertia and familiarity. We all know people who prefer to go to the same restaurant and order the same entrée when they dine out; we also know others who prefer new experiences and choose to try unfamiliar establishments and exotic dishes. The latter tend to be more open and willing to change than the former. If an organization is populated primarily by people who favor familiarity, a change agent must recognize that sparking change will be more difficult at first.

Age is another factor that can affect some people's willingness to change. Humans tend to be creatures of habit. Older people's habits are more deeply embedded. However, change agents should resist being biased around age or assuming that an organization that has many older workers will be especially change resistant. Stereotypes are generally rooted in some truth, but there are always counterexamples. At the companies with which I work, I have known many older workers who love to learn, grow, and evolve—and who are always up for the challenge of finding new ways to work.

After recognizing and evaluating these predictable tendencies, entrepreneurial leaders have several ways they may try to motivate change. I've described this hierarchy of motivations in *The 10 Laws of Trust* as a way to consider the most powerful and likely approaches to produce durable change.[6] Each of them can motivate people, but they vary in the extent to which team members will buy into the change and whether they will have a lasting impact on their behavior. I focus on five potential motivations:

Force: The warden of a prison has the ability to get inmates to do limited actions, but actions motivated by the use or threat of force are temporary at best. To change others' behaviors in a more permanent way, a leader must help team members *want* to transform, so that they are doing so voluntarily. Changes driven by force never work in a business environment and rarely have any lasting effect once the force is removed.

Fear: Many companies institute change when the business starts to decline. In these instances, the changes may be accompanied by layoffs as the organization tries to shrink expenses to match declining revenues. In this kind of environment, team members may accept change because they are afraid. Entrepreneurial leaders recognize that threat-induced change usually lasts only about as long as the threat is imminent.

Reward: Companies frequently try to incentivize change by changing their compensation plans. This is especially common among sales forces. For instance, if a company's strategic focus shifts from acquiring new customers to obtaining more revenue from existing clients, it might change the commissions and bonuses paid to sales representatives so that they don't receive commissions until a customer has stayed on board for six months (making them focus on onboarding and retention) or increasing the commission rate for reorders. But compensation is only one way to reward people. Recognition, celebration, and advancement may be less effective in the short run but are more durable in the long run.

Duty: A change initiative that relies on people's belief in an important cause or mission can have powerful and enduring results. Consider how dramatically Americans' behavior changed during World War II. Men volunteered for hazardous overseas duty; women performed grueling manual labor in factories; investors purchased low-returning war bonds; consumers cut back on purchases of goods needed by the military. Appealing to one's sense of mission is only possible when a deep affiliation exists between an individual and an institution. When that bond is strong, it is usually because of the meaning that has come from a commonly held mission. When the hard preparatory work has been done to find meaning, the willingness to change tends to be high. Indeed, it no longer even feels like change but rather becomes the excitement of winning something that matters.

Love: The most powerful motivator for durable change is love. In the book *Fearless: The Undaunted Courage and Ultimate Sacrifice of Navy SEAL Team SIX Operator Adam Brown*, author Eric Blehm tells a tale that is, above all, a story of the power of love in a young man's life lost to drug addiction. The firm, consistent, but demanding love of his wife, Kelley, brought Adam back from the brink to the highest levels in the elite team of SEALs.[7] A more mundane example of the motivating influence of love can be seen with the television program *The Biggest Loser*, which features overweight people attempting to lose (in some cases) hundreds of pounds of body weight. Participants tend to cite the same motivation for the punishing regimen of exercise and dietary restrictions they are undertaking. "I'm doing it for my family," they typically say. "I want to be around to watch my children grow up." People are willing to sacrifice when moved by love. When people feel real love for an organization, it is usually for their coworkers or a boss. And when the connection is deep, they may be willing to change in significant ways without the lure of personal reward or the fear of loss. Where love exists, change can be permanent.

As leaders learn to be more effective in precipitating change, they discover that the surest way to bring people along is to change their own behavior and establish visible new habits: to *show* the way rather than simply telling others how to do it. This realization comes from the steps taken to become an entrepreneurial leader—making changes in one's own operating system to become more trustworthy. At the granular organizational level, this means if you want people to start meetings on time, you'll have to start meetings before latecomers have arrived. If you want follow-up reports, you'll have to report on your own commitments. If you want customer service to improve, you'll have to handle the occasional customer complaint.

Years ago when I was in a position to influence change at Trammell Crow, I wanted our partners to become more connected with tenant concerns and complaints as a part of developing customer loyalty. I urged partners to stay in close touch with their tenant base. After a few weeks of this, my assistant quietly pulled me aside. She pointed out that I *never* spoke with tenants myself, so perhaps I didn't have as much credibility on this issue as I'd like. My encouragement seemed hypocritical. Taking her critique to heart, I set up weekly phone calls with tenants to see how they were reacting to the service we provided. Not only did I learn a lot, but word soon got around that I really did care about tenant concerns. I began modeling the change I wanted to see, and many others began to follow.

In every instance of organizational change I have led or witnessed, the changes were painful, and it would have been easier in the near term to avoid them. But in each case, the outcome of change has been superior to allowing the status quo to linger. As organizations become larger and more successful, inertia is powerful, and hierarchies and habits develop around the status quo. It takes an entrepreneurial leader to overcome inertia and to replace fear with a sense of duty and connection to the team. He or she must push the organization to confront the reality that the future will be unlike the past and that change, therefore, is not optional.

RECAP

▶ Driving durable change is the essential job of the entrepreneurial leader and should be a top priority at every
stage.

▶ Entrepreneurial leaders must recognize that resistance
to change is a part of the human condition and use the
principles of managing change to lead others.

▶ When people believe in an organization's mission, the
momentum for change is easier to develop.

EPILOGUE

F or the past quarter century, at the end of each semester I've given a "Last Lecture" to my class at Stanford's Graduate School of Business. Many universities have a Last Lecture series in which they ask a professor to speak on this topic: "What wisdom would you try to impart to the world if you knew it was your last chance?" The concept caught fire in 2007 after Randy Pausch, a professor of computer science at Carnegie Mellon who'd been diagnosed with terminal pancreatic cancer, gave a talk that went viral. After he spoke, he was given a standing ovation from the hundreds assembled—and the resulting YouTube video inspired millions more to reflect on what final messages they would leave before they depart this life.

My less-compelling valedictory has evolved over years of delivery, discovery, and rediscovery. I draw on my experiences as a former real estate *executive* (where I have deal stories to tell), as an angel *investor* (where I've had failures and successes), as an *entrepreneur* (where I've nurtured some fledgling businesses and failed with others), as a *father* (where I've learned and taught life lessons), as a *husband* (where I've navigated a lifelong partnership through its ups and downs), as a *board member* (where I've offered and received advice), and as a *teacher* (where I've learned to love all of my students, whether or not I like all of them all the time). From these disparate journeys, I've distilled best-practice maps for business and for life, which I offer in condensed form to my students.

In this lecture, my basic approach draws on a concept from Frederick Buechner, the American essayist and theologian. I've read many of his works, and the message I've taken from them is this: in all our dreaming, planning, hoping, and striving, our lives will ultimately find joy and meaning if we succeed in discovering only three things:

1.   A person to *be*
2.   Someone to *love*
3.   A work to *do*

A book offering the route to becoming an entrepreneurial leader may be irrelevant to finding someone to love. However, it may legitimately offer guidance on two out of Buechner's three vital imperatives. Becoming an entrepreneurial leader demands personal growth, no matter where you start—and along the way, you'll likely discover more about the person you'd like to be and the meaningful work you want to do. (I'd also offer reasonable odds that if you do these two things well, you'll be a happier, more confident, and more optimistic person—the kind who may do well in finding someone to love.)

Being an *entrepreneur* is a particularly energizing form of leadership in which one lights fires, innovates, creates new ventures, and plays a role vital in the economy and in society. However, most ventures fail—and sooner than later. And few pure entrepreneurs are adept at creating durable enterprises ready to be picked up by a next generation with the vision to turn them into institutions.

While *presiding* over established institutions is also demanding and vital, it is largely a question of learning the ropes, knowing people and mastering rules, then applying them with wisdom. No trivial task. Indeed, society demands the continuity and predictability of well-run institutions—and those who do this work are important pillars of society.

Finally, other important leaders are adept *managers* and administrators, handling complexity with great skill, leading team members to on-time, on-budget outcomes vital to the life of an enterprise. Managers play key roles in our lives.

So while pure entrepreneurship, governance, and management are all worthy pursuits that yield societal benefits and gratifying careers to those who perfect them, it is the entrepreneurial leader who plays the role of change agent in securing enduring enterprises that can eventually be managed and led by others.

Entrepreneurial leadership does not depend on being an entrepreneur first. It requires a mind-set, a set of skills, a general adherence to best-practice maps, and the ability to survive on the mountain after dark.

We need more entrepreneurial leaders. Indeed, our politicians could take a page from the book of entrepreneurial leaders who must meet current and future payrolls, who must consider consequences beyond a next election cycle, who must anticipate the world of our children and grandchildren, and who must translate their positions of power and influence to be able to deliver—and live with—results that will last.

Indeed, to those who've developed the mind-set, the self-talk, the courage, the grit, the wisdom, and the skills to manage this most challenging form of leadership, I tip my hat. I've learned from you, mimicked you, struggled to do as well as you. I hope this book plays a small role in helping a new generation climb toward this summit—one that represents what, to my mind, is the highest form of leadership.

ACKNOWLEDGMENTS

E*ntrepreneurial Leadership* is my second book, and working on it provided a vivid reminder that publishing is a team sport. Although my name is on the cover, many people contributed to the volume you're now holding.

My agent, Shannon Marven at Dupree Miller in Dallas, helped me navigate the world of publishers and introduced me to HarperCollins Leadership, where I was fortunate to find people who understood the need for a book like this.

I'm indebted to the entire team at HarperCollins Leadership: Jeff James, Tim Burgard, and Amanda Bauch. I also owe a big thanks to copyeditor Jamie Chavez for not only correcting the manuscript but especially for scrutinizing quotations and fine-tuning footnotes.

I have been extremely fortunate to have colleagues and friends at Franklin Covey who have been enthusiastic supporters of this project. To Bob Whitman, Scott Miller, and Drew Young go my deepest thanks.

I never let a day go by without feeling grateful for my seven children, whose personal and professional accomplishments give me so much happiness. All seven of them have married spouses for whom I am also grateful. During the months I spent writing the book, I relied on two of them for special assistance. My daughter-in-law Alex Peterson and son-in-law Kevin Mitchell helped manage the project—keeping track of deadlines, managing relationships, and keeping the team aligned and informed. I am grateful to Alex and Kevin for their assistance.

Daniel McGinn, an editor at *Harvard Business Review*, proved an ideal collaborator as I revised my original manuscript. Dan and I spent long Saturdays side by side, working to elicit and frame the right stories, streamline the structure, and increase the clarity of the lessons. I enjoyed his competence and professionalism.

Mark Fortier and Lisa Barnes of Fortier Public Relations and Ken Gillett of Target Market Digital did superb work in helping bring my work to the attention of readers.

My executive assistant, Jean Bair, helped me contact the former colleagues and students whose stories fill these pages to ensure the recollections I share are true and accurate.

My Stanford colleagues Peter Robinson and Charles O'Reilly spent a Fourth of July weekend reading and offering incisive comments on the manuscript; I am deeply indebted to them for helping me improve it. Clint Peterson and Jake Kastan also read drafts and provided invaluable feedback.

My wife, Diana, read the manuscript more times than I can count, each time providing gentle redirection and encouragement. Diana has my deepest gratitude, and my love.

Finally, thank you to the students who have filled my classrooms over these past twenty-seven years at the Stanford Graduate School of Business. I learn from you and am inspired by you, every day. Although I've been fortunate to invest in and help launch many companies, I'm convinced my work as a teacher will be my most lasting professional legacy—and that the lessons I've taught will live on and be improved upon through the lives of my students.

—Joel Peterson
Palo Alto, CA
October 2019

NOTES

The World Needs More Entrepreneurial Leaders

1. Although I experienced the Asurion story firsthand as an investor, many of the details on how Kevin Taweel and Jim Ellis grew Road Rescue into Asurion are recounted in Stanford Graduate School of Business Case #E-167, "Asurion," revised December 17, 2012. This case was originally authored by Alicia Seiger under the supervision of H. Irving Grousbeck and revised by Arar Han. I used details from this in my retelling of Asurion's story.
2. Stanley McChrystal, *Team of Teams* (New York: Portfolio, 2015), 225.
3. Although I know Amy Errett firsthand, I also consulted and relied on a Stanford case study when writing about her leadership: Peter Kelly and Jessica Morgan, "Madison Reed," Stanford Graduate School of Business, Case #E-553, October 5, 2015.
4. Bryce Hoffman, *American Icon* (New York: Currency, 2013), 57–58.
5. Hoffman, *American Icon*.

Build Trust: Step 1

1. Jim Collins, "Level 5 Leadership: The Triumph of Humility and Fierce Resolve," *Harvard Business Review*, July–August 2005, https://hbr.org/2005/07/level-5-leadership-the-triumph-of-humility-and-fierce-resolve.
2. Bernard Tate, "Boston Marathon Hero Awarded Soldier's Medal," US Army (website), April 28, 2014, www.army.mil/article/124781/boston_marathon_hero_awarded_soldiers_medal.
3. Adam Nossiter, "A Shot, a Glimpse of an AK-47, and U.S. Servicemen Pounced on Gunman on Train to France," *New York Times*, August 22, 2015, www.nytimes.com/2015/08/23/world/europe/americans-recount-gunmans-attack-on-train-to-france.html.

Build Trust: Step 2

1. Ray Dalio, *Principles* (New York: Simon & Schuster, 2017), 451.
2. Anson Dorrance, *The Vision of a Champion* (Chelsea, MI: Sleeping Bear Press, 2002), 49.
3. Stephen Covey, *The 7 Habits of Highly Effective People* (New York: Simon & Schuster, 2016), 80.
4. Andrew Saltoun, in a phone interview with the author, February 25, 2019.
5. Saltoun, interview.
6. Bonny Simi, in a phone interview with the author, May 13, 2019.
7. Simi, interview.
8. Simi, interview.

Build Trust: Step 3

1. This story is based on Guy Raz's interview with Andy Dunn on the NPR program *How I Built This with Guy Raz*, January 21, 2019, www.npr.org/2019/01/18/686640146/bonobos -andy-dunn.
2. Tom Peters, "A Brand Called You," *Fast Company*, August 31, 1997, https://www .fastcompany.com/28905/brand-called-you.
3. Peters, "A Brand Called You."
4. Adam Grant, *Give and Take* (New York: Viking, 2013), 3–4.
5. Grant, *Give and Take*.
6. Arianna Huffington, *Thrive* (New York: Harmony Books, 2014), 1.
7. Arianna Huffington, email message to author, September 4, 2019.
8. Clifton Leaf, "Dream Catcher," *Fortune*, November 30, 2016, https://fortune.com /longform/arianna-huffington-thrive-global-company/.
9. Huffington, email message to author, March 1, 2019.

Build Trust: Step 4

1. Clayton Christensen, James Allworth, and Karen Dillon, *How Will You Measure Your Life?* (New York: Harper Business, 2012), 2.
2. Leo Tolstoy, *Anna Karenina*, 1877, 1.
3. Christensen, Allworth, and Dillon, *How Will You Measure*, 72.
4. Christensen, Allworth, and Dillon, *How Will You Measure*, 79–80.
5. From a speech to the National Defense Executive Reserve Conference in Washington, D.C., November 14, 1957.
6. David Brooks, "The Moral Bucket List," *New York Times*, April 11, 2015, www .nytimes.com/2015/04/12/opinion/sunday/david-brooks-the-moral-bucket-list.html.

Create a Mission: Step 1

1. Zach Mercurio, "What Every Leader Should Know About Purpose," *HuffPost*, February 20, 2017, www.huffpost.com/entry/what-every-leader-should-know-about -purpose_b_58ab103fe4b026a89a7a2e31.
2. Matt Weinberger, "Microsoft CEO Satya Nadella Says Bill Gates' Original Mission 'Always Bothered Me,'" *Business Insider*, February 21, 2017, https://www.businessinsider .com/microsoft-ceo-satya-nadella-bothered-by-bill-gates-mission-2017-2.
3. Michael J. Coren, "Facebook's Global Expansion No Longer Has Its Mission Statement Standing in the Way," *Quartz*, June 22, 2017, https://qz.com/1012461 /facebook-changes-its-mission-statement-from-ing-its-mission-statement-from-sharing -making-the-world-more-open-and-connected-to-build-community-and-bring-the -world-closer-together/.
4. Mark DeWolfe Howe, ed., *Holmes-Pollock Letters: The Correspondence of Mr. Justice Holmes and Sir Frederick Pollock, 1874–1932*, 2nd ed. (Cambridge, MA: Belknap Press of Harvard University Press, 1961), 109.

Create a Mission: Step 2

1. "The World's Greatest Goal Achiever," John Goddard, 1924–2013: World-Renowned Adventurer, Explorer, Author, Lecturer (website), www.johngoddard.info/obituary.htm.

2.   www.johngoddard.info.
3.   Rebecca Trounson, "John Goddard Dies at 88; adventurer fulfilled most of childhood goals," *Los Angeles Times*, May 21, 2013, https://www.latimes .com/local/obituaries/la-xpm-2013-may-21-la-me-john-goddard-20130521 -story.html
4.   John Doerr, *Measure What Matters* (New York: Portfolio, 2018), 7.
5.   Winston Churchill, "Blood, Toil, Tears and Sweat, 1940" National Churchill Museum (website), www.nationalchurchillmuseum.org/blood-toil-tears-and -sweat.html.
6.   Yousuf Karsh, *Winston Churchill*. 1941. Photograph. Yousuf Karsh (website), karsh.org /photographs/winston-churchill/.
7.   James C. Collins and Jerry I. Porras, "Building Your Company's Vision," *Harvard Business Review* (September–October 1996): 65–77.
8.   Gary Hamel and C. K. Prahalad, *Competing for the Future* (Boston: Harvard Business School Press, 1989).
9.   Edwin Locke and Gary P. Latham, *Goal Setting: A Motivational Technique that Works* (Englewood Cliffs, NJ: Prentice-Hall, 1984).

Create a Mission: Step 3

1.   Paul Millerd, "Decoding McKinsey's Culture of High-Performance: Building A Lasting Firm," *StrategyU*, https://strategyu.co/decoding-high-performance-mckinsey -company/.
2.   Douglas Martin, "Marvin Bower, 99; Built McKinsey & Co.," *New York Times*, January 24, 2003, https://www.nytimes.com/2003/01/24/business/marvin-bower-99 -built-mckinsey-co.html.
3.   Marvin Bower, *The Will to Manage* (New York: McGraw-Hill, 1966).
4.   Bower, *Will to Manage*, vi–vii.
5.   Bower, *Will to Manage*, 3.
6.   Bower, *Will to Manage*, 18.

Create a Mission: Step 4

1.   Cecil Dijoux, "Edgar Schein: Organizational Culture and Leadership," *#hypertextual* (blog), January 17, 2013, https://thehypertextual.com/2013/01/17/edgar-schein -organizational-culture-and-leadership/.
2.   SAS Institute Inc., "Jim Goodnight: Co-Founder & Chief Executive Officer," *SAS .com*, www.sas.com/en_us/company-information/leadership/jim-goodnight.html.
3.   Jenn Mann, "The SAS Story: Building and Sustaining a Unique Culture," *HuffPost*, August 22, 2014, www.huffpost.com/entry/the-sas-story-building-and-sustaining-a -unique-culture_b_5700489.
4.   Patty McCord, "How Netflix Reinvented HR," *Harvard Business Review* (January– February 2014).
5.   Netflix, "Netflix Culture," *Netflix.com*, https://jobs.netflix.com/culture.
6.   Chris Sloan, "JetBlue: Is Its Jettitude Culture Enough to Carry It into the Future?" *Airways News*, March 14, 2014.
7.   Bob Sulentic, in a phone interview with the author, March 26, 2019.

Secure a Team: Step 1

1. Jim Collins, *Good to Great* (New York: Harper Business, 2001); Jim Collins, "First Who . . . Then What?" JimCollins.com, www.jimcollins.com/concepts/first-who-then -what.html.

Secure a Team: Step 2

1. Waldman, Peter. "A Sex Scandal Rocks Stanford's Business School," *Bloomberg Businessweek*, October 7, 2015, https://www.bloomberg.com/news/features/2015-10 -07/a-sex-scandal-rocks-stanford-s-business-school.
2. Deepak Malhotra, "15 Ways to Negotiate a Job Offer," *Harvard Business Review*, April 2014.
3. Dale Carnegie, *How to Win Friends and Influence People* (New York: Simon & Schuster, 1936), 3.
4. Martin E. P. Seligman, *Flourish* (New York: Free Press, 2011), 30.
5. Seligman, *Flourish*, 33–34.
6. Dave Maney, "The Valley needs a business Mr. Rogers . . . and I think I found him," *Venture Beat*, September 15, 2018, https://venturebeat.com/2018/09/15/the-valley -needs-a-business-mr-rogers-and-i-think-i-found-him/.
7. Nitin Nohria, "Commencement 2016: Dean Nitin Nohria" (video), Harvard Business School (website), May 27, 2016, https://www.hbs.edu/about/video.aspx?v=1_rhnkrl7o. For transcript see Nitin Nohria, "Dean Nohria Addresses the Class of 2016," Harvard Business School (website), May 26, 2016, https://www.hbs.edu/about/leadership/dean /Pages/message-details.aspx?num=10571.
8. David Needle, "Humor in the Workplace," *Gentry*, September 2017, editiondigital .net/publication/?i=434159#%7B%22issue_id%22:%22434159 %22,%22view%22:%22articleBrowser%22,%22article_id%22:%222864921 %22%7D.
9. Connie Dorigan, "Could Humor Be Your Key to Success?" Dorigan & Associates (website), April 26, 2017, dorigan.com/career-advice/could-humor-your-key-to-success.
10. Norman Cousins, *Anatomy of an Illness: As Perceived by the Patient* (New York: W. W. Norton, 1979), 33.
11. Cousins, *Anatomy*.

Secure a Team: Step 3

1. Mark Harris's story is based on an interview with the author, August 18, 2018.
2. Ben Horowitz, *The Hard Thing About Hard Things* (New York: Harper Business, 2014), 105.

Secure a Team: Step 4

1. Kim Scott, *Radical Candor* (New York: St. Martin's Press, 2017), 68.
2. Andrew Hoffman, *Builder's Apprentice* (Ann Arbor, MI: Huron River Press, 2010).
3. Andrew Hoffman, "Firing Someone: What They Don't Teach You in B-School," *Harvard Business Review*, April 15, 2010, https://hbr.org/2010/04/have-you-ever-fired -someone-le.
4. Hoffman, "Firing Someone."
5. Hoffman, "Firing Someone."

Deliver Results: Map 1
1. Peter B. Kyne, *The Go-Getter: The Story That Tells You How to Be One*, http://www .fullbooks.com/The-Go-Getter.html.
2. W. H. Murray, *The Scottish Himalaya Expedition* (London: J. M. Dent, 1951).
3. Annie Duke, *Thinking in Bets: Making Smarter Decisions When You Don't Have All the Facts* (New York: Portfolio, 2018), 89–90.
4. Daniel Kahenman, Dan Lovallo, and Oliver Sibony, "Before You Make That Big Decision . . .," *Harvard Business Review*, June 2011, https://hbr.org/2011/06/the-big -idea-before-you-make-that-big-decision.
5. Malcolm Gladwell, *Blink: The Power of Thinking Without Thinking* (New York: Little Brown, 2005), 13–14.

Deliver Results: Map 2
1. Frank V. Cespedes and Daniel Winefurter, "More Universities Need to Teach Sales," *Harvard Business Review*, April 26, 2016.
2. Zig Ziglar, *Zig Ziglar's Secrets of Closing the Sale* (New York: Berkley Books, 1984).
3. Carmen Nobel, "Professional Networking Makes People Feel Dirty," *Working Knowledge*, Harvard Business School, February 9, 2015, hbswk.hbs.edu/item /professional-networking-makes-people-feel-dirty.
4. Daniel H. Pink, *To Sell Is Human* (New York: Riverhead, 2012), 2.

Deliver Results: Map 3
1. Sulentic, interview.
2. PON Staff, "10 Hard-Bargaining Tactics to Watch Out for in a Negotiation," *Program on Negotiation* (blog), Harvard Law School, July 1, 2019, www.pon.harvard .edu/daily/batna/10-hardball-tactics-in-negotiation/.
3. Alison Wood Brooks, "Emotion and the Art of Negotiation," *Harvard Business Review*, December 2015, https://hbr.org/2015/12/emotion-and-the-art-of -negotiation.
4. *Wall Street*, directed by Oliver Stone (1987; Hollywood, CA: American Entertainment Partners and Amercent Films).

Deliver Results: Map 4
1. Andy Dunn, in correspondence with author, date unknown.
2. Dane Stangler, *The Economic Future Just Happened*, Ewing Marion Kauffman Foundation, July 9, 2009, https://www.kauffman.org/-/media/kauffman _org/research-reports-and-covers/2009/06/theeconomicfuturejusthappened .pdf.

Deliver Results: Map 5
1. Jack Welch, *Winning* (New York: HarperCollins, 2005).
2. Stephen Denning, *The Leader's Guide to Storytelling: Mastering the Art and Discipline of Business Narrative* (Hoboken, NJ: Wiley, 2005).
3. Peter Senge et al., *The Fifth Discipline Fieldbook: Strategies and Tactics for Building a Learning Organization* (New York: Doubleday, 1994).

Deliver Results: Map 6

1. Patrick Lencioni, *Death by Meeting: A Leadership Fable about Solving the Most Painful Problem in Business* (New York: Jossey-Bass, 2004).
2. Douglas Stone, Bruce Patton, and Sheila Heen, *Difficult Conversations: How to Discuss What Matters Most* (New York: Penguin, 2010).

Deliver Results: Map 9

1. "Geoffrey West," Santa Fe Institute (website), www.santafe.edu/people/profile/geoffrey -west.
2. Geoffrey West, *Scale: The Universal Laws of Growth, Innovation, Sustainability, and the Pace of Life in Organisms, Cities, Economics, and Companies* (New York: Penguin, 2017), 403.
3. West, *Scale*, 396.
4. Patty Mulder, "Griener Growth Model," Toolshero, https://www.toolshero.com /strategy/greiner-growth-model/#targetText=Larry%20Greiner%20assumes%20 that%20an,development%20phase%20of%20an%20organization.
5. Comment made in author's Stanford class, date unknown.

Deliver Results: Map 10

1. In a debate in the House of Commons with Philip Snowden, First Viscount Snowden, on June 23, 1925.
2. An observation by Victor Frankenstein in the 1818 novel *Frankenstein*. Shelley, Mary, *Frankenstein* (Mineola, New York: Dover Books, 2013).
3. Arthur Brooks, "How a Think Tank Measures the Impact of Ideas," *Harvard Business Review*, March–April 2018, https://hbr.org/2018/03/aeis-president-on-measuring-the -impact-of-ideas.
4. Bob Whitman, in a phone interview with the author, February 28, 2019.
5. Whitman, interview.
6. Joel Peterson, *The 10 Laws of Trust*, exp. ed., (Nashville: HarperCollins Leadership, 2019).
7. Eric Blehm, *Fearless: The Undaunted Courage and Ultimate Sacrifice of Navy SEAL Team SIX Operator Adam Brown* (Colorado Springs, CO: Waterbrook, 2013).

INDEX

ABOUT THE AUTHOR

Joel Peterson is the chairman of JetBlue Airways and the founding partner of Peterson Partners, a Salt Lake City-based investment management firm. Joel is on the faculty at the Graduate School of Business at Stanford University and has been since 1992. After three careers, four decades of marriage, and seven kids, in addition to demanding roles as CFO, CEO, chairman, lead director, adjunct professor, founder, author, entrepreneur, and investor, Joel is often sought as a mentor and coach by leaders and aspiring leaders.